THE THEATRE STUDENT SERIES

The Theatre Student

Costuming

 THE THEATRE STUDENT SERIES

The Theatre Student

COSTUMING

*Berneice Prisk
and
Jack A. Byers*

Published in 1970 by Richards Rosen Press, Inc.

PUBLISHED BY

RICHARDS ROSEN PRESS, INC.
NEW YORK, N.Y. 10010

Standard Book Number: 8239-0147-5
Library of Congress Catalog Card Number: 70-75261
Dewey Decimal Classification: 792

Published in 1970 by Richards Rosen Press, Inc.
29 East 21st Street, New York City, N.Y. 10010

Copyright 1970 by Berneice Prisk and Jack A. Byers

Revised Edition

Manufactured in the United States of America

ABOUT THE AUTHORS

Berneice Prisk, Professor of Drama at San Jose State College, San Jose, California, has designed and executed costumes for an impressive number and variety of theatrical productions. The list, which totals about 360 productions for both adult and children's theater, television, dance, opera, and musicals, involves costumes of practically all periods and many countries.

Before joining the faculty of San Jose State College in 1948, she taught at Northwestern University, where she had previously taken B.S. and M.A. degrees, at Allegheny College, at the State University of Iowa, and at the University of Michigan. She is a member of the American Educational Theatre Association, the Children's Theatre Conference, and the American National Theatre and Academy. For several years she was Costume Editor of *Players Magazine*. Her extensive writings in the field include *Stage Costume Handbook* and numerous articles and book reviews.

Jack A. Byers, Associate Professor of Drama at San Francisco State College, San Francisco, California, has created costumes for more than one hundred productions, including musicals, operas, and classical and contemporary plays. A graduate of San Jose State College, with B.A. and M.A. degrees, he did advanced study at the University of Oregon. He has taught at Utah State University, Michigan State University, and the University of California at Santa Barbara. He is a member of the Children's Theatre Conference and the American Educational Theatre Association, and has served as an officer in the Northern California District of the latter organization.

Julie Harris in Anastasia *produced by Hallmark Hall of Fame.*

Contents

Contents

The Theatre Student

Costuming

CHAPTER I

The Script

The creation of stage costumes begins with the script for operas, musicals, plays, staged readings, or dance concerts. Reading and rereading many times may be desirable to assimilate the author's intentions concerning the characters, references to costume, time, locale, and any special demands the playwright has included. Charting the appearances of the characters scene by scene will show who is in each scene, the char-

acters appearing together, scenes having crowds, and how often each character appears. This charting will indicate places where certain characters have fast costume changes. (It is wiser to know this before planning rather than getting caught short of time at the first dress rehearsal.)

The sample chart given here for *The Music Man* shows the scenes in which the whole ensemble appears, the scenes includ-

MUSIC MAN CHARACTER CHART—WOMEN

Character	Act I											Act II						
	1	2	3	4	5	6	7	8	9	10	11	1	2	3	4	5	6	7
Ethel		x			x	x					x	x			x		x	x
Eulalie		x			x	x					x	x			x		x	x
Bertha		x			x	x					x	x			x		x	x
Maude		x			x	x					x	x			x		x	x
Mrs. Squires		x			x	x					x	x			x		x	x
Alma		x			x	x					x	x			x		x	x
Mrs. Paroo		x		x	x					x	x		x	x	x			x
Marian		x					x			x	x	x	x	x				x
Gracie		x		x		x					x	x			x			x
Zaneeta		x		x		x					x	x			x			x
Girls (10)		x			x		x				x	x			x			x

13

MUSIC MAN CHARACTER CHART—MEN

Character	Act I											Act II						
	1	2	3	4	5	6	7	8	9	10	11	1	2	3	4	5	6	7
Marcellus		x			x	x					x				x	x	x	x
Newsreader	x																	
Hix		x			x	x					x	x	x	x	x		x	x
Salesman	x																	
Brett		x			x	x					x	x	x	x	x		x	x
Mayor Shinn		x			x			x		x	x						x	x
Conductor	x																	
Townsman		x			x						x				x			x
Charlie	x													x	x	x	x	x
Townsman		x			x						x				x			x
Salesman	x																	
Dunlap		x			x	x					x	x	x	x	x		x	x
Harold Hill	x	x	x		x	x	x	x	x	x	x	x	x	x	x	x	x	x
Salesman	x																	
Boy		x			x		x				x	x			x			x
Squires		x			x	x					x	x	x	x	x		x	x
Salesman	x																	
Townsman		x			x						x				x			x
Winthrop		x		x	x					x	x			x	x		x	x
Townsman		x			x		x				x				x		x	x
Tommy		x			x		x	x			x	x			x			x
Farmer		x			x						x	x			x			x
Boys (6)		x			x						x				x			x

ing small groups, and the places where Marian, in particular, has little time to make a costume change. If the number of actors is fewer than the number of characters, some actors may play several parts. The chart will show where this is possible. For example: The Salesmen in the opening scene can double as Townsmen in the street scenes with a moderate costume change. These are shown together on the chart. From the chart it is evident that Act I, Scenes 2 and 11 and Act II, Scenes 1, 4, and 7 include the whole ensemble. Also, since Marian must wear a costume in Act II, Scene 3 different from the one in Act II, Scene 2, this necessitates a quick change. The chart also shows that the writers have allowed for chorus costume changes.

Costumes may either be designed so that changes can be made in a minimum of time, or designed so the garments can be worn in layers. In a multiple-scene play it would be unusual to have an intermission between each scene; ordinarily one or two intermissions will suffice. Therefore, a character at the end of one scene may need to make a costume change and reappear at the beginning of the next scene almost immediately. Eliza in *My Fair Lady* is an excellent example of this. Because of the changes in her character as she becomes more and more ladylike, costume changes are necessary, but she is seldom offstage long enough to do this at leisure. Her costumes must be planned so that they can be put on and removed easily.

Often the playwright may make references to costume in the dialogue. It would be disconcerting to the audience to hear "Mary is wearing a red dress today" and then have Mary enter in a yellow print. The dialogue and the costume must tally, either by designing the costume to match the dialogue or, in some cases, matching the dialogue to the costume.

A lapse of time between acts or scenes may indicate costume changes. For example: Act II. Ten years later. If the same characters are included it would indicate a change of costume. In some early periods a ten-year lapse of time might not reflect a change of costume style; in other periods, it would. Also, the change of costume helps to show the audience that time has elapsed. Characters may age throughout a play and would seldom wear the same clothing as they grew older. The activities of each act may determine the costume. If a woman enters after a tennis match, then is going to a dinner party later, she would undoubtedly wear a different outfit. If the locale, climate, or setting differs during the play, additional costumes might be necessary. An analysis of each character according to age, physical attributes, personality, nationality, occupation, wealth, social status, physical activity, relationships with others, and focal scenes is desirable before progressing with plans for the costumes.

The play may need to be read several times before assimilating all the data contained therein. First, know the plot, mood, and general atmosphere, then take copious notes on the details.

The designer's and director's combined interpretations result in costumes intended to carry out the playwright's ideas. A production sometimes may stray far afield from the playwright's intentions when an offbeat or bizarre treatment is attempted. For example, a production of a Shakespearean play might be conceived in "far-out" modern dress, or with all the characters in a basic style such as tights and leotards. Designers and directors can sometimes come up with some very unusual ideas for experimentation. The finished production is the result of the setting, lighting, and costume designer's ideas incorporated into the total production as envisioned by the director. If all personnel involved aim in the same direction, the result should be a product with unity. If not, the production may seem to go off in all directions at once. Amicable communication between the director and designers is essential to an effective production, the give and take of ideas arriving at a unified whole. The director who can blend effectively the ideas of the designers without domination by director or designer is very skillful and makes his efforts and those of his co-workers look good. Frequently directors and designers differ in their ideas. Often it is the designer who will be required to curtail his ideas to some extent and come to an agreement with the director for the success of the production.

All productions should be started with a meeting of all designers with the director before anyone proceeds with his own concept. This meeting is a clearing ground to set the style. Is the play to portray a naturalistic effect? Is it to be stylized? Is it a modern-dress treatment of a period piece? Or something else? Out of this meeting must come the decisions to determine the style the costume designer will use to create his apparel. A play reflecting a normal everyday household of people is likely to be treated in a natural style. The characters may be dressed as closely as possible to a photographic picture of the real-life people of the play's period. In contrast, a musical comedy might exaggerate the costumes of the characters and the period. For example: The gangsters in *Guys and Dolls* are the most extreme of all gangsters; Harold Hill in *The Music Man* is the very symbol of all traveling men; Mary in *Little Mary Sunshine* is the epitome of sweetness and light; or you might have an allegorical character representing a symbol of Justice or Charity.

Color also enters into the initial agreement among the designers involved. In some situations the same person may design both sets and costumes. This creates a unity in itself. When costumes and settings are designed separately a conference to plan the color palette is essential. Since one is not complete without the other, and neither is complete without stage lighting, they must harmonize. Usually this cooperation can be depended on, since the total effect will be a combination of all efforts. The understanding of stage lighting is most important, as the enhancement of both sets and costumes is dependent on it.

The responsibility of the director in relation to the costumer is essentially one of communication. He should be able to express to the costumer his ideas with regard to characterizations, any specific uses he might make of costume in stage business, the needs of the characters for specific details of costume such as: practical pockets, removal of costume on stage, necessary accessories exclusive of those mentioned in the script, omission of any mentioned in the script, rigorous action affecting the costume, padding to change the physique of the actor, or other stage action influencing or affecting the costumes. An agreement should be reached with the costumer about the number of costumes desirable and necessary for each character and the number of characters involved if variable, such as crowds, armies, and the like. All the factors must be considered at this point, such as the time involved in costume changes or references to costumes in the script.

If the director does not provide the necessary information the designer should, for his own protection, ask about any aspects of the costumes that might affect the design or execution. It is far better to know the problems in the planning stage than to have them appear suddenly at a later date, causing much extra labor and effort. The director who says, "Can Lord John be padded as a fat man?" the day before dress rehearsal is likely to get a cold stare in response. The costume should be finished by this time and will have been fitted to an unpadded actor. The costumer can scarcely be expected to remake the whole costume at this late date.

The costumer's responsibility is to provide costume designs and plans early in the rehearsal period—or before—and the finished costumes in time for the first scheduled dress rehearsal. It is important that he communicate his ideas to the director for confirmation. If changes are necessary along the route of construction, the director should be consulted. It is wise for the costumer to consult with the director on style, color, and fabric for each costume.

If cast changes are made or characters added or removed during the rehearsal period, the costumer must be notified immediately. Lack of communication on this aspect can cause considerable hard feelings between director and costumer.

The casting of a production is the prerogative of the director. The costumer, however, must have fittings with each and every character, regardless of importance. Since it is the director who works in close association with the actors, the costumer must depend on his cooperation to communicate to the actor the relationship of his costume to his acting. Therefore, the actor must cooperate by being available for fittings. Professional actors would quickly lose their jobs if they did not appear, but amateur actors often have the attitude that they are conferring a favor on the costumer when they appear for a fitting. The actor should somehow realize that both he and the costumer will look better in the production with his cooperation and that he can do a better job of acting if he also looks the part. Costumers should guard against using up any more of the actor's time than is necessary for fittings and adjustments. They should keep in mind that the actor is also spending much time and energy in rehearsals; fittings are an extra chore.

Normally the costumer cannot fully complete his designs until the director has cast the production. In many roles the physique of the actor may have considerable influence on the style and design of the costume. Many designs have ended up in the wastebasket because they would not be properly effective on a particular actor. It is usually wise for a designer to keep his designs flexible and open to change until the casting is complete. Frequently it becomes the costumer's responsibility to make the actor look thinner, fatter, taller, or shorter to carry out the director's conception of the physical aspects of the character. In the chapter on design there are references to methods of altering the actor's appearance by emphasis on length or width. The costume can do many things, but often ingenuity is strained to the utmost when superimposing a character upon the actor's body. For example: It would be almost an insurmountable obstacle if a short, fat man were to be cast as Abraham Lincoln, a fat person as an underfed character, or a tall man as a 10-year-old boy. Adding weight to an actor is far easier than subtracting it.

No one aspect of a production is independent of the others. The costumes are a result of the communication of the costume designer with the director together with the cooperation of the actors involved. A costume is not complete until it is on an actor on a stage in the setting appropriate to the play and lighted in a proper manner. The setting provides the background against which all costumes are seen, and the lighting not only makes them visible to the audience but enhances them as well.

Research. Before designing, information and ideas about the period and locale of the play are gathered to give a better understanding of the type of clothing worn in any period or region. Some knowledge of the background of the play is desirable: the period in which it was written and the place in which the action occurs. Depiction of historic events requires knowledge of those events; perhaps even research into what a historical character actually wore at that time.

The art and customs of a period tells us not only what people wore but *how* the clothing was worn and handled. Viewing costume in relationship to its architectural background gives the designer a better understanding of the clothing.

When a play requires costumes of a country that has a society differing in structure from our own, some knowledge of it will be of help in selecting appropriate styles for the characters of the play. Remember that not all cultures share our accepted norms of dress. Traditions accepted in Western clothing may be quite different in another country. For example, black is not the traditional color of mourning in all societies.

The primary concern, of course, is to learn about the types of costume required by the play. Each historical period has its own styles. Although it is not always necessary or desirable to practice strict adherence to a period's fashions, the costumes should be a fairly true reflection of the period; they may, however, be simplified and/or exaggerated for the stage.

Research is a means of gathering ideas for costume design. Any library will have periodicals and books useful to the costumer. Fashion magazines are valuable for research into stylish dress of the 20th century, and some libraries contain fashion periodicals dating back even earlier. Magazines devoted to the home, such as *Ladies' Home Journal,* may contain illustrations of middle-class people and everyday clothing. Sears Roebuck and Montgomery Ward catalogues yield information concerning every conceivable type of garment. Newspapers and magazines such as *Life* and *Look* often contain drawings or photographs of historical figures and events: coronations, religious investitures, and so forth. One of the best sources of national dress is the *National Geographic.*

The kinds of books most useful for costume research are those dealing with the overall history of a period or country, reproductions of the art of a period or a painter, and books on the history of costume. Recent years have seen an amazing increase in the publication of books devoted to costume. Many are superbly illustrated and can greatly help the costumer in his research. These books usually deal with the entire history of costume or are devoted to the coverage of a single historical period. The latter type of costume book is preferable, for it will give much more information. However, no history book of costume completely covers any period. It is advisable to consult several works so that a broad knowledge of a period's fashions may be obtained.

Museums are another source of research material. Paintings and sculpture can be of great help to the designer as he assimilates the mood and feeling for the period as well as the clothing style and color. Many museums, such as the New York Metropolitan Museum of Art or the Los Angeles County Museum of Art, contain collections of clothing. These actual garments are of help in giving the designer the best possible idea of what was worn and its appearance, including colors, textures, and construction details.

One source of research must be mentioned, since it is available to all: family memorabilia. Faded tintypes, school annuals, old wedding gowns—all can give a vivid portrait of what was worn in the not-too-distant past, particularly for such productions as *Our Town* or *My Fair Lady*.

In doing research, it is a good idea to make as many notes and sketches as possible. Make a record of any information that might be of use and organize it. One good way is to maintain a notebook or file for the production in which sections are devoted to such items as foundation garments, hats, shoes, dresses, accessories, trimmings, colors, and fabrics. Write down the source of any information so that you can refer to it when desired.

The process of research is completed when the costumer is able to apply the information he has gained to the problems of the production. Most contemporary plays require little assembling of clothing details. Historical plays require more research, as do those using regional or national costume. From research, the following knowledge is gained:

1. The dominant silhouettes of the period or locale. Each historical period is characterized by certain silhouettes, as for example the women's bell shape of the American Civil War period.

2. The popular fabrics and colors. Each period had its own concept of what was fashionable in color and texture. The use of colors and fabrics is important in giving the correct appearance and drape to the costumes. Colors may need to be modified for the production. *Oklahoma!* is probably more effectively costumed with much brighter colors than actually were used by the Oklahoman pioneers. The authentic fabrics of a period may not be available or may be too expensive for use. The costumer then searches for the modern, inexpensive fabric that will have the same draping quality and appearance.

3. The fashionable trimmings and accessories. Often the use of carefully chosen trimmings and accessories will greatly help in giving the correct period look to a costume. A man's sack suit of 1900 is little different from what is worn today. The use of such items as watch fob, spats, and stickpin will help to ensure a period look.

Also gained from research is a knowledge of the practical and aesthetic functions of dress. These are of aid in determining the correct type of costume for a character. Practical functions would include modesty, warmth, and protection. The well-clad medieval lady wears voluminous garments to conceal the body as well as to give warmth, necessary when living in a stone castle. The medieval knight, in his suit of armor, covers the cuirass with a heraldic tabard to protect the armor from rust and also, through the heraldic device, to identify himself. Costume has also an aesthetic function in that it helps to alter the body into the popular ideal figure. Corsets and padding are the primary means of accomplishing this, but the actual shape of garments (sleeves and so forth) may be of further importance.

Examining photographs of past productions of a play can be of some use in showing how another designer interpreted the clothing of a period. These photographs may also help in determining the types of garments most effective for a character or group of characters.

A production reflects the ideas and attitudes of the director, actors, and designers regarding the play. Unity results when all elements are in harmony. Costumes, then, are most effective when they have been planned for a particular production; that is, when they are keyed to the setting, lighting, and acting. Copying of either authentic garments of the past or costumes from other productions of a play is not recommended. They may not be in keeping with the production style and, further, costumes copied from other sources are bound to suffer in comparison. An imitation is never as good as the original! Especially to be avoided is the copying of costumes from past productions, particularly those that might be familiar to the audience. Comparison is inevitable. For example, any production of *My Fair Lady* that employs black and white costumes for the Ascot scene will be compared to the original Broadway production or the motion picture version. It is far better to evolve costumes geared to your production. The designs may not be as striking but they will be more satisfactory because they will have suitability to the production rather than echoing a previous one.

Achieving originality in costume is possible even with limited design ability. Imagination is desirable, but more important is the careful choice of garments and the simplification and/or exaggeration of the chosen style. In designing the historical costume, search for that style most in keeping with the character and production. Slavish adherence to authenticity is seldom required, but the costume should have the overall shape and effect of the period. The colors and fabrics should be carefully chosen. Details used should be large enough to be recognizable; small ones will be merely distracting. Selection of detail and some exaggeration will give the costumes the effect desired at the distance from stage to audience.

In addition to the aesthetic considerations given the costumes (mood, choice of period, and locale), there are also practical considerations. Budget, time, manpower, and facilities should be taken into account when designing.

Budget. The budget determines how lavish or rich-looking the production may be. It is a factor in deciding whether the costumes are to be velvet or muslin; whether emphasis is to be placed on richness of fabric or on line and color. More ingenuity may be needed when working within a limited budget but this does not mean that costumes need be dull or uninteresting. Good effects can be achieved with limited funds, but careful consideration needs to be given to how the available money is to be spent and how the costumes can make the best use of the budget.

Time. Most productions rehearse from four to six weeks prior to performance. In this time, the costumer builds or assembles the costumes to be used. Planned carefully, the costumes will all be completed on time. It may be desirable to keep the costumes as simple as possible. The use of the same pattern for a number of costumes; restriction of hand-sewn trimming; use of any stock costumes available: All this can aid in making sure that the costumes are completed on time.

Manpower. The costumes should be designed so that they can be built by the available manpower. Consideration should be given to the number of people available for construction and to the sewing experience of those people. With a large crew, costumes may be fairly complex in style but it would be futile to design costumes beyond the abilities of the crew. With few people available for construction, it might be better to simplify the costumes: relying on color and line for effect, rather than placing emphasis on detail. Another important factor is the experience of the crew. Costume workers may be volunteers with little or no practical experience, or they may be accomplished seamstresses. With experienced help there should be little difficulty in realizing fairly complex designs. Often a school's Home

Economics department is willing to build the costumes. This provides valuable experience for students and is a godsend to the costumer. Remember that the department may be prepared to handle only a certain amount of work. The designs should not demand too much of this work force. Often the crew will consist of volunteer help not directly connected with the school or theatre, such as mothers or friends of the cast. Under these circumstances, the work is often done in private homes. It is important to spell out carefully what is to be done and, if necessary, how it is to be done. The design, and the sketch of it, should be clear and within the building experience of the worker.

A community can be made conscious of the theatre-costume needs and activities of its drama-producing groups in several ways. Voluntary helpers can work on the costume construction of productions—and this includes men as well as women. Many costumes need mechanical and even engineering skills—construction of armor, animated masks and animal costumes, art techniques in painting and decorating, cobbler's skills for period shoes, metal workers for swords and accessories. Many costumes need the combined skills of a designer and an electrician, mechanic, painter, engineer, or others too numerous to mention.

Another method of making a community aware of the costume activity is the solicitation of items that can be used for costumes. The following items are some that are useful:

Cast-off or broken jewelry and beads to use as stage jewelry or trimmings

Old fur coats, stoles, jackets to be used as they are or cut up for trimming

Bedspreads, draperies, curtains, or clothing to be used or remade into other things

Feathers, ribbons, or trimmings of any kind

Hats to be used or remade

Shoes, period types especially, or other standard styles (High-buttoned or laced shoes for men or women are a real asset.)

A note in the program of a production or in a newspaper saying this type of donation will be welcome can bring in a wealth of usable items. Often the public is delighted to find some place to unload these things. Always accept everything thankfully. If there are unusable items, they can be passed along to someone else or disposed of later. This is good publicity, as it makes the public aware of the drama activity.

Facilities. The space and equipment at the disposal of the costume crew is also important. With no facilities, the show may have to be costumed with rented costumes or, if the budget is not large enough for that, the costumes may have to be built in the homes of cast members. If this is the case, it would be important to keep the designs as simple as possible, planning on the use of little or no special techniques such as dyeing, armor-making, and so forth. It is desirable to have excellent facilities and an abundance of equipment, but many a show has been costumed in the confines of a closet-sized room. Even a fairly elaborate musical can be costumed with limited facilities and much enthusiasm.

Each of the practical considerations mentioned above affects the design of a show. If the budget is severely limited but there is plenty of time and manpower available, then the designer is free to plan costumes that rely on the ingenuity of the workers, rather than achieving effects through the purchase of expensive fabrics or accessories. For example, it is possible to gain the appearance of velvet through a careful dyeing and texturing of cheaper fabrics such as flannel or terry cloth. Money can thus be saved but there is a greater demand on time and facilities. Without workers to build costumes, or without facilities and equipment, the costumer may have to resort to either renting or borrowing costumes. Following is a list of some of the costume-rental companies:

Brooks Costume Company, 16 West 61st Street, New York, N.Y.

Eaves Costume Company, 151 West 46th Street, New York, N.Y.

Intermountain Costume Company, 30 Constitution Building, Salt Lake City, Utah

Minneapolis Costume Company, Minneapolis, Minnesota

New York Costume Company, 10 West Hubbard Street, Chicago, Illinois

Van Horn & Son, 811 Chestnut Street, Philadelphia, Pennsylvania

Western Costume Company, 5335 Melrose Avenue, Hollywood, California

Consult the classified telephone directory of the nearest large city for additional firms.

These practical considerations, then, are kept in mind during the design process. They are restrictions but need not be a hindrance to the designer. They serve to give a focus to the designs, and pride may be taken in costumes that were produced within the budget and in the given time for construction.

MINIMUM OF COSTUME CHANGES

The initial impression of a character is created by his costume. The audience identifies him with his costume. A change of costume can be confusing to an audience unless the character has been firmly established. Any additional costumes should bolster the effect created by the initial one or serve to further the development of the character. Musicals and many plays, such as those of Shakespeare, will often suggest more than one costume for each character. Costume changes should occur only when necessary, when demanded by the script or when desirable for furthering character. Not only will this help the audience to identify the players but it eases the workload for the costume crew and is saving on the budget. One effective device frequently seen in both professional and nonprofessional produc-

tions is to restrict complete costume changes to the principals only, giving supporting characters partial costume changes to suggest lapses of time or changes of mood and locale. Musicals do this frequently. Basic costumes may be designed for the chorus that, with additions, will suggest the various scenes. For example, the chorus girls in *Carousel* might be costumed in basic cotton dresses. The addition of jackets and hats will serve for the opening number and a change to aprons and hair ribbons would be suitable for the clambake. A careful use of color, line, and texture is necessary so that the costumes will be suitable for a number of scenes. Examples of how a costume may be altered through a change of accessories is given in the chapter on construction.

COLOR, LINE, AND TEXTURE PLOTS

Achieving a total harmony in the costuming of a play involves the plotting of three major elements of costume: color, line, and texture. The designer considers their qualities and how each may be of use to the total appearance of the production as well as in each individual costume.

Color Plot. An audience notices color more than any single detail of a costume. Color tends to be more dominant than even the lines or textures of a costume. It may cause a character to stand out from all others or it can be used to make a character recede into the background. Color enhances both the style and mood of the production. It creates and maintains interest in character. It is used to direct the attention of the audience. It is the designer's most powerful tool.

The associations an audience makes with color, and the ability of color to enhance the physical and psychological aspects of character can be used to advantage to enhance both character and play.

The effect of a color is dependent on a number of factors, such as intensity (increasing brilliancy or saturation of a color gives an increasing effect of both agitation and prominence); relationship to other colors (widely different effects can be achieved in varying color combinations); and the texture of the colored fabric (colors used on shiny fabrics are more dominant than on dull fabrics).

Dominant colors such as white and red should be used sparingly, for they direct attention to themselves and are often irritating to the eye when used in large quantities. White, a color associated with innocence, reflects light and can be very distracting on stage. (A light beige will pass for white at a distance and is more pleasing.) In costuming any actor in white, remember that it enlarges the figure. The easiest way to suggest large feet is to put the actor in white shoes! The most adaptable colors on stage are grays or muted tones. Black, the color of mystery and death, is generally not considered to be bold. It can be extremely dominant on stage, however, especially when contrasted with such colors as red or yellow. It tends to minimize size and is an extremely effective accent color.

The colors of comedy are the warm colors (yellow, red, orange) because they have an immediate association with happiness, warmth, and, sometimes, violence. They are stimulating, exciting colors that arouse the emotions.

Tragedy is usually cloaked in cool colors (blue, green, violet) because they suggest a dignity and spiritual quality. Cool colors can often be used to cause a jarring or exciting effect. Cool colors tend to decrease size, whereas warm colors seem to enlarge it.

Evolving the Color Plot. In choosing the colors for a production, consider first that it is necessary to give unity partly through color. This does not mean that all costumes should be the same color. That would result in a drab, artificial-looking production! It does mean a careful working out of the colors to be used: making sure that they are harmonious, unless color clashes are necessary to further the action of the play.

The style of production will determine the choice of colors. A representational production would call for a realistic use, whereas a presentational or slight exaggeration in style might employ a more limited range. For example, a group of students in a realistic drama might be costumed in dark, drab hues, whereas a musical comedy version of a classroom scene would call for bright, intense colors.

One effective way to evolve the color plot is to follow this procedure:

1. Determine the colors to be used in the costumes for the total production. Perhaps a wide range of colors will be used or a more restrictive color scheme might be employed, such as a dominance of warm colors with accents of one or two cool colors. Choose not only the colors but also the particular shades and tints of each. Avoid the use of a color scheme chosen more because of current color fads than because of the demands of the script; it will only call attention to itself. An example of establishing the overall color plot would be the choice of intense, primary colors for *The Taming of the Shrew* combined with muted shades of the same tones. All the colors can then be brought together, unified, by the use of black for accent on all costumes.

2. Once the overall color scheme has been determined, decide which colors are to be used on the principal characters. Normally, these should be the more dominant colors, those used less extensively in the other costumes or more intense tones. Generally, one color should dominate in a costume, with one or two other colors used as accent. The use of more than three colors in a costume, regardless of the proportions used, tends to produce a cluttered effect.

3. Determine the colors for the other characters. Often these may have been used for accent on the costumes of the principals. Avoid repeating exactly the same color on

more than one character as it may confuse the audience in identifying the characters.

Additional considerations in the choice of color:

1. *Groupings*. Often a director deems it necessary to group his actors in a definite arrangement, such as a tableau. In this case, colors should be carefully selected so that the grouping will be pleasing to the eye; the colors should be harmonious and well balanced.

2. *Relationships*. It is sometimes desirable to show the physical or psychological relationship of characters. This can be done easily through the repetition of color. For example, Romeo might be dressed in blue with accents of rose and white. Juliet might be costumed in rose with accents of blue and white. Thus the characters are visually united. The use of one color for all members of an army is another example of color being used to show a relationship.

3. *Clashes*. If a character is opposed to another, this may be demonstrated by costuming the two in clashing colors. The opposition of the two street gangs in *West Side Story* may be made visually clear and exciting by costuming the two groups in clashing colors.

In selecting color, search carefully for the correct shade or tint. The variations of each color are limitless; there is one that will be right for the character. Choose the accent colors with equal consideration. When all colors are selected, discuss the proposed color plot with the setting and lighting designers. The lighting should enhance the costumes. The colors of the costumes should be harmonious with the setting.

Line Plot. A costume is composed of a series of lines, which, when arranged, depict the garment of a particular shape, containing the details of style. The overall shape or outline of a costume is the silhouette. Most historical periods offer a choice for both male and female. The costumer chooses the one most suited to the character and production. The historical silhouette may be modified or distorted but it is important that it remain recognizable, for it is this shape that enables the audience to determine the period of the play. To maintain unity, the costumer will use only a few silhouettes in a production, working variations on each. This helps to give unity to the costumes.

Another determining factor is the size of the theatre. Subtle effects, so effective in a small arena theatre, may be lost in a large auditorium. The larger the theatre, the more pronounced the silhouette must be, and the more exaggerated must be the use of line. For any theatre, the costumer needs to use an exaggeration of line. A costume should be "larger than life." Details that are too small will only confuse the audience. Everything about the costume must be purposefully done and with simplicity, so that the effect remains uncluttered. The necessity for exaggeration can be illustrated by the fact that a red-and-white-striped fabric will, in most theatres, appear as solid pink. At a distance, the stripes blend into each other; the striped detail is lost because it is not large enough to carry the distance from actor to spectator.

A third factor in the choice of line and silhouette is the actor. A decision should be made whether it is desirable to flatter the actor's figure or to capitalize on any of his deficiencies. Attention is given to the matter of proportion. In general, it is bad design to divide the body into equal proportions. A garment that uses unequal proportions is more flattering. A line placed at a joint (skirts ending at the knee or sleeves ending at the elbow) gives an awkwardness to the body.

Fourth, the movement of the actor needs to be considered. Actors are seen in motion and their costumes are seen from many angles and in many positions. A tight, constricting skirt might be quite lovely when a winsome actress is standing erect, but the same skirt can become ugly when seen in motion. Consider the traditional costumes worn in ballet. They are designed so that the body always appears graceful, and the costumes do not take on their greatest beauty until they are seen in motion.

Lastly, line must be correlated to the colors and textures of the costume. Bold colors and textures demand equally bold lines. Softness in line requires soft, subtle fabrics and colors.

Each type of line suggests emotional qualities and has an effect on the appearance. Briefly:

1. Horizontal lines suggest dignity and repose. They are suited to a character whose position in life is well assured. Horizontal lines widen the body; a horizontal line on a costume tends to cut the body at that point. Because of this, avoid a strong horizontal line low on the body, unless a shortening is deliberately desired.

2. Vertical lines also suggest dignity, but they give a person more stature. They elongate and slim the figure. Strength and virility may be communicated by the use of vertical lines.

3. Diagonal lines serve to direct the attention from one detail in the costume to another. In use, they may be slimming and are effective in balancing either horizontal or vertical lines.

4. Angular lines are, of course, a combination of diagonal lines. They suggest unrest and tension and are especially effective on nervous or mischievous characters. The traditional costume of the court jester is composed of a multitude of angular lines.

Straight lines are considered masculine and have a severity, whereas curved lines are soft and feminine. It would be impossible, of course, to use only one type of line in designing. A costume is composed of many lines, and each may be handled in a slightly different way. Yet one type of line will dominate in a good costume design to make the clearest statement about the character.

Related to the concerns of line and sil-houette is the use of patterned fabrics in costumes. It is usually best to keep patterned fabrics at a minimum onstage, to avoid a cluttered effect. If the use of a pattern is desirable to indicate either historical period or character, care should be used in choosing a pattern that will project at a distance. A very small pattern may look like a textured fabric at a distance. Worse is the patterned fabric that is too small or too large for the figure wearing it. Choose patterns in proportion to the actor and with the size of the theatre in mind. Floral patterns are usually considered feminine, although some drapery fabrics are available with large floral patterns that can be extremely effective on men. A striped fabric will fatten or slim the figure, depending on whether the stripes run horizontally or vertically. Stripes have a bold, hard quality. They suggest a sternness of character and are just fine on governesses and stern maids. Plaid fabrics usually enlarge the figure, and care must be taken to select a plaid that will be effective at a distance. Small patterns, checks, stripes, and plaids can frequently be used in place of a plain fabric. The motif not visible from a distance may provide texture, highlights, and shadows to give more variety among a group of plain colors.

Texture Plot. Full realization of a design is partly dependent upon the costume being made of a fabric that will drape as indicated by the design and move with the character in a graceful and appropriate manner. Some costumers select their fabric first, putting ideas down on paper after the textures have been selected. Other costumers visualize the costume first, selecting the fabric after the design has been completed. Selection of fabric is governed by two factors: the weight or draping quality of the fabric and the surface or texture appearance. Fabrics that fall in heavy folds are usually heavy in weight, such as velvet or corduroy. Such fabrics give an appearance of dignity, especially when seen in motion. Lightweight fabrics may fall into either stiff or soft folds. Chiffon and organdy are both light fabrics, but the former has fluid draping quality, whereas the latter falls into stiffer folds. The chiffon is useful in suggesting a billowy, ethereal quality.

Of the countless number of fabrics currently manufactured, three general types of surface effects are available. First, many fabrics have a dull, light-absorbing surface. Corduroy and woolens are fabrics with such a surface. They may be either rich or plain-looking, but all have a somber quality and may be used to denote a serious person. Secondly, fabrics may have a shiny surface. These light-reflecting fabrics, such as satin or chintz, are primarily frivolous and feminine. They are the fabrics of comedy. When used in small amounts (cape linings, collars and cuffs, and so forth) they may denote richness in a somber, dignified person. Lastly, fabrics may have a glittery surface. Such fabrics may have a metallic embossing; metallic threads woven into the fabric; or may be studded with jewels or sequins. Such fabrics are well suited to fantasy characters, such as the fairies in *A Midsummer Night's Dream*.

In designing a show, it is usually best to work with a number of textures, striving for variety in fabrics. A production costumed all in velvet is just as dull as one costumed all in muslin! Just as one color should dominate in a costume, so one fabric should be predominant, with other fabrics used for contrast.

A classic example of a costume utilizing color and texture contrasts is the traditional Santa Claus suit. The dominant color is red and the fabric is light-absorbing. Serving as contrast is the white fur trim and the shiny black boots. Nothing dull here! The costume makes an emphatic theatrical statement.

CONSIDERATIONS FOR THE ACTOR, SINGER, DANCER

The audience comes to the theatre to be entertained by a story: a story told by the performer. All visual elements are subordinate to the actor relating the story. The performer may be actor, singer, or dancer. The audience is there in the theatre to pay attention to this person. The costume that he wears helps to emphasize the performer. Good design has been achieved when the costume helps the actor become the character. But this good costume goes further. It allows the character to perform the actions and movements required of him by the play, enhanced by the costume.

Just as any painting contains a focal point, the face of the actor is his focal point. It is the face that the spectator is primarily interested in and that should be emphasized. This sounds simple and logical enough, but it can pose problems for the costumer. Many a beautifully designed large-brimmed hat has been discarded following the first dress rehearsal because the audience would not be able to make out the expressions on the shadow-covered face of the actor. Any hat or costume detail that might obscure the features of the face should be carefully designed or eliminated to avoid the problem.

Actors can adjust to garments far removed from contemporary clothing. But the costumer designs with the actor's comfort in mind. The actor can learn to manipulate unusual styles of costumes with sufficient rehearsal. Most historical styles fit more tightly than modern clothing. Often a tight fit is essential for a proper period look. However, the costumer can adjust slightly: retaining the tight look but keeping the costume loose enough to forestall continual complaints from the performer. How much adjusting needs to be done is dependent on the demands of the role. For any performer who must undergo strenuous action, it is best to design a costume that has some ease in its fit: a costume not totally dependent on fit for its effectiveness.

Actors. Actors should not have to worry about costume while onstage. The costume should permit movement without requiring excessive adjusting and securing. Many details of historic costumes look lovely in paintings and in sketch form but may become quite ugly onstage if the actors are unable to handle them. Skirts with long trains can be treacherous to any actress ill trained in their manipulation. A large bustle may seem very appropriate for Julie's first appearance in *Carousel,* but the action required of her would suggest that it had best be eliminated or, at least, minimized in size. Action required of a particular character may influence the designer in his planning of the costume. For example, Lady Macbeth might well be costumed in a long, trailing skirt requiring her to hold it so that she can move. But the action of the play requires her to make an entrance, following the smearing of the grooms with blood, with the blood-stained daggers in her hands. What is to be done with the skirt? In this instance, it would probably be decided that the costume should have a floor-length skirt with little or no train.

Actors often must make very fast costume changes, and the costumes must be designed to allow this. The costumes of *Auntie Mame* need to be spectacular but equally important is that they must be designed for rapid changes. Many costumes must be designed with rugged use in mind. Fights, death scenes, and so forth require costumes that will withstand the strain. If an actor is to be dragged across the stage, a chiffon gown is impractical. Furthermore, a white costume is probably out unless the costumer can afford the cleaning bills! So the costumer thinks not only of the character but also of what the character does. The costume must permit and enable this.

Singers. Considerations in the design of costumes for singers are basically the same as for actors. Care must be given that there is nothing tight around the neck; a feeling of constriction can hamper the vocal efforts of all but the most experienced singers. The bodice should allow for diaphragm expansion, and sometimes the fit must be looser.

Dancers. The strenuous and expansive movements of dancers call for care in the planning of the costumes. They should permit full body freedom and be free of any decoration that might interfere with the required movement. The choice of undergarments is important. They should not bind or constrict and, if visible to the audience, should be in keeping with the rest of the costume. Bodices for both female and male dancers should be snug-fitting but not tight. The bodice should usually present a smooth torso with a low waistline (just above the hip line). This assures that the waist will appear normal even when the dancer is involved in a lift or extension. Skirts should be full and the length manageable by the dancer. Tight sleeves usually hamper movement unless extra fullness (as in a gusset) is given in the armscye. Trousers should be either form-fitting or full enough to allow for the leg movements, with a high crotch. Shoes for dancers need to be lightweight. Fortunately, especially designed dancers' shoes are available, inexpensive and adaptable to most historical periods. Accessories should be kept to a minimum and designed with the dancer's movements in mind. Any item that might pose a problem to the dancer should be given sufficient rehearsal time.

GETTING THE IDEAS DOWN ON PAPER

The rendering or sketch of the design is the blueprint of the costume to be built. It is a guide in construction and is useful to director and actor, for it shows the visual appearance of the character. The sketch may be a work of art or not, depending on the drawing ability of the designer. It should be emphasized that the design needs to have clarity, but that it is not necessary that it be suitable for framing. The ideas for the costume are put down on paper in as clear a form as possible, and these are used in achieving the more important goal, the full realization of the costume.

The drawing of the human body is difficult for some people. Time and frustration may be saved by drawing several figures and, through tracing, using these for all designs. Or they may be traced from books or magazines and the costume drawn over the figure. It is best to use poses suitable for the design, and the body should be of average proportions. Use of the tall fashion figure, for instance, will give a different appearance to the costume than it will probably have on the actor.

Plates I and II are drawings of average-proportioned male and female figures, in suitable poses for costume design. These may be traced or made larger or smaller by transferring the drawings to squared paper of another size.

Sketches are more effective when done in color. Any media may be used, such as water color, gouache, acrylics, or colored pencil. The use of color in the sketch gives a better idea of how the costume will look than if only pencil or pen and ink are used.

It is helpful to attach swatches of the costume fabric to the design. This enables anyone looking at the sketch to determine the color and texture as well as the lines of the costume.

DIRECTOR-COSTUMER CONFERENCE

After the designer has put his costume ideas into sketch form, he meets with the director to discuss the designs. Each sketch should be explained to the director so that he has the best possible idea of how the costumes will look onstage. Some directors have difficulty in visualizing the sketched costume as it will appear on the actor. The design should be explained carefully with attention given to any aspect of the costume that might not be evident in the sketch.

The costumer seeks approval of the designs before proceeding to construction. The director may request some changes. Any problems related to costume should be solved at this time. It is important that this meeting result in the director's obtaining a clear idea of how the actors are going to look, and that the designer know what the director expects from the costumes.

There should be agreement on character. The costume should bolster the actor's interpretation and not be misleading. For example, Marian, in *The Music Man,* must look every inch the prim librarian and not like an Ohio femme fatale.

Does the costume help the actor's movement? The action required of the character should be considered when evaluating the design.

Does the costume harmonize with other costumes? Spreading out the designs on a table will enable the director and designer to look at all of them at once, to see if the proper relationships have been established.

The costumes should relate to all other aspects of the production, creating a unified whole. They should be in harmony with the settings, lighting, and properties. It is especially important that there be no conflicts either in style or in color.

BUDGETS AND ESTIMATES

In the average school or producing organization it is necessary to estimate the cost of a production before any purchasing can be done. The entire cost of the costumes sometimes must be figured out before the designs or casting are complete. Because of this all items must be included. Following is a check list of the kind of expenses normally associated with the costuming of a production.

1. All fabrics necessary for the construction of any costume, including linings, underpinnings, fabrics for trimmings, hats, headdresses, and accessories

2. Notions or findings such as thread, fasteners, bias tape, seam tape, and elastic

3. Trimmings: braid, feathers, flowers, jewels, ribbon, buttons, and other purchasable decorations

4. Shoes: purchase of shoes, footwear, hose, tights, or materials if they are to be made

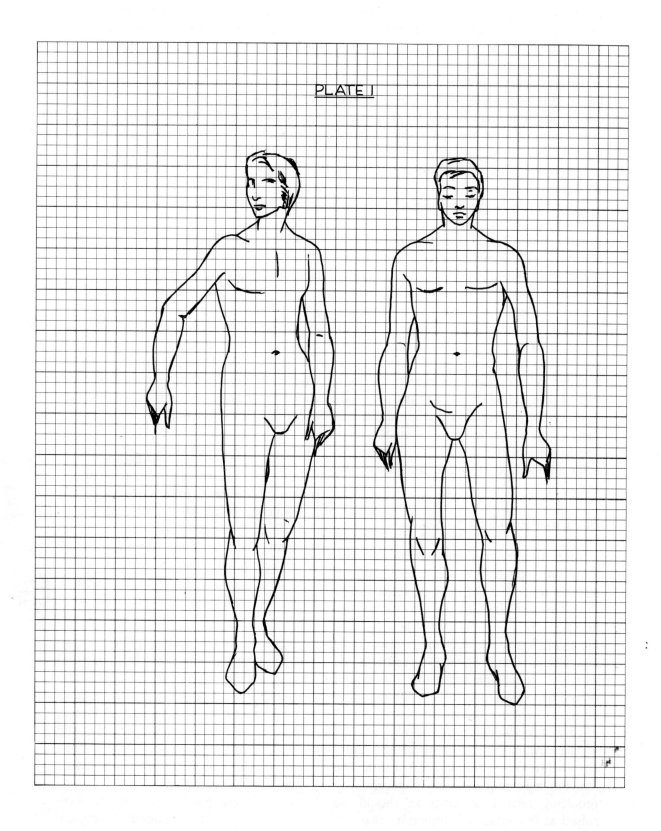

PLATE I

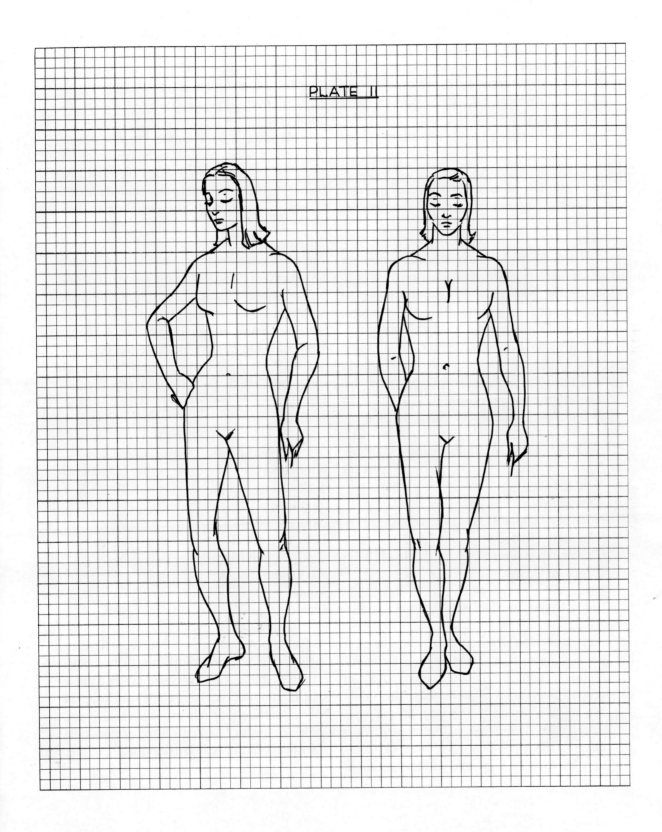

PLATE II

5. Hats and headdresses to be purchased or materials for their construction

6. Padding materials for changing body shapes

7. Accessories such as gloves, purses, canes, parasols, etc., to be purchased or constructed

8. Rental charges for items to be rented

9. Paint, mask, or armor supplies

10. Dry cleaning and laundry charges for the costumes after the production has closed

To make an estimate of a large number of similar costumes the easiest method is to figure out one costume, carefully using an average-size person to estimate yardage, then use that as a norm for the whole group. Usually what is saved on one costume can be used to eke out a more expensive costume, and the actual cost will work out all right. The addition of approximately 10 percent as a cushion to allow for emergencies is al-

money where it will do the most good. Shopping with limited funds requires know-how and careful planning in order to avoid unnecessary purchases. If there are costumes or parts of costumes on hand or available without cost, this, of course, reduces the total cost.

Following is an estimate for *The Music Man* plus the actual cost of the costumes for the production. In most cases there will be some variation between an estimate made before purchasing and the actual costs. It is wiser always to purchase slightly under the estimate; then the money saved can be used for some items that might run higher. It isn't always possible to get more money. Organizations have a habit of limiting their funds.

The estimate and actual cost listed here were the result of figuring out the probable cost per costume first. Because the purchasing must be done according to the type of items purchased, each costume was divided into its components, pooling all the costumes together.

Music Man Estimates

Shoes and hose	15	percent
Yardage	25	"
Trimmings	10	"
Notions	10	"
Hats and Headgear	10	"
Clothing purchase	15	"
Paints and dyes	2	"
Rental	5	"
Laundry and dry cleaning	8	"

Music Man Actual Costs

Shoes and hose	11	percent
Yardage	20	"
Trimmings	10	"
Notions	10	"
Hats and Headgear	10	"
Clothing purchase	20	"
Paints and dyes	5	"
Rental	5	"
Laundry and dry cleaning	9	"

ways a good insurance. The technique of a good estimate is to allow enough for moderate expenditure but not so much that the cost of the show is more than the funds available. Frequently the cost of the costumes must be tailored to the money available. In this case, figure out what is necessary for each costume and use the available

These percentages, of course, will vary with different types of shows. The above estimates and actual costs are taken from a specific production, using some wardrobe on hand, particularly shoes, headgear, and some costumes. The items listed are possible classifications for any production.

CHAPTER III

Costume Construction

Measurements. When the designs for the costumes are completed and the actors chosen, it is necessary to get their measurements in order to construct, rent, or purchase the costumes. If costumes are to be rented, the rental company will usually furnish a measurement chart to be filled out for their use. If the garments are to be purchased, the sizes of commercial garments worn by the actors are often sufficient. This refers to shoe, hose, dress, shirt, trousers, coat, or hat sizes. For shoe purchase, a footprint of the actor is very useful. Have the actor stand on a piece of paper and draw around his stockinged foot. Use this pattern of the foot when purchasing shoes or slippers, which may not run true to commercial shoe sizes. Actual measurements may be necessary in addition, however, since different makes of garments vary in size. If costumes are to be constructed, a rather full set of measurements is needed. The number of measurements depends on the style of the costume: a loose sacklike garment needs fewer measurements than a fitted one. Plate III gives a diagram of the human body and a list of the measurements necessary for the average costume. Also on this illustration are included head measurements necessary for the construction of hats and wigs.

The measurements for a complete production can be incorporated into a single chart for men and women, or made into individual charts for each actor. If there are many costume construction workers the individual charts have some advantages. The disadvantage is that they seem to get lost more easily than the master chart. Perhaps the use of both is the best. Taking measurements too loose rather than too tight is safer. A garment can always be taken in when being fitted, but it might not be as easy to let it out if it's too tight. Take the measurements over a minimum of clothing, mark the natural waistline with a cord, and be sure they are accurate. The body diagram on Plate III shows the correct placing for taking measurements.

Fabrics. The selection of the fabrics for the construction of stage costumes requires a knowledge of fabrics, the fabric vendors available, and imagination in visualizing the effect of a fabric from the audience viewpoint. For the best results a designer should do his own shopping. His mental picture of the effect he desires is difficult to communicate to another person. The manner in which a fabric drapes and its texture can be seen only with a large piece and not from small samples. A patterned fabric may look quite different at a distance as compared to a close view. From a distance the following changes may occur: a small pattern may show up as a plain color with interesting highlights and shadows, a large pattern may have one color or motif predominant, a shiny surface may look lighter in color, a pastel may look faded, bright colors may vibrate, or the effect just isn't the same as in a closer view. An excellent idea is to hang the fabric over the end of a counter then walk away from it noting the variations as the distance increases. The cost of the fabric is usually important and may need to be

PLATE III

MEASUREMENTS

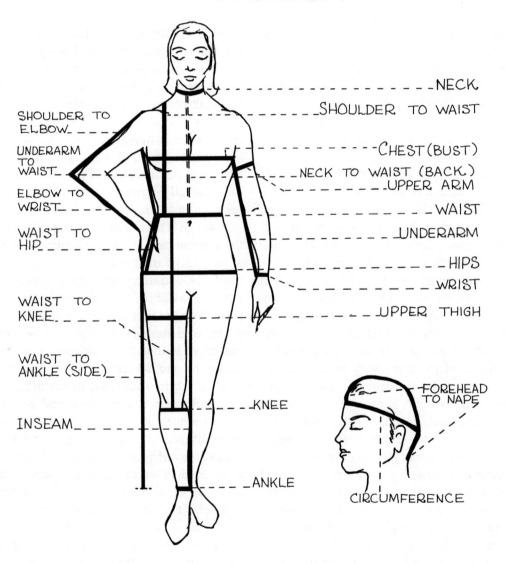

NECK

SHOULDER TO WAIST

CHEST (BUST)

NECK TO WAIST (BACK)
UPPER ARM

WAIST

UNDERARM

HIPS

WRIST

UPPER THIGH

SHOULDER TO ELBOW

UNDERARM TO WAIST

ELBOW TO WRIST

WAIST TO HIP

WAIST TO KNEE

WAIST TO ANKLE (SIDE)

INSEAM

KNEE

ANKLE

FOREHEAD TO NAPE

CIRCUMFERENCE

tailored to a limited budget. The unlimited budget doesn't exist for the average production. Therefore, look at fabrics in all available shops. Pick up samples of the likeliest to compare with other shops. When all swatches have been gathered, spread them out with the designs and fit the whole together. At this time, rather quick decisions must be made in order to return to the store for the desired purchases while the fabric is still on hand. If large quantities are needed, a vendor with sufficient stock on hand must be found.

When looking for stage fabrics use all available sources. Department store yardage departments are one source; inspect also drapery and upholstery fabric stores, drapes and curtains and bedspreads in thrift shops, secondhand clothing shops, war surplus warehouses, and other similar sources. There are companies that specialize in theatrical fabrics. These stores often have fabrics not found in the average yardage shop. Following is a list of a few of these:

Dazian's, 142 West 44th Street, New York, N.Y.; 125 North Wabash Street, Chicago, Illinois; 726 South Hoover Street, Los Angeles, California

Dance Art Company, 222 Powell Street, San Francisco, California

Hollywood Fancy Feather Company, 512 South Broadway, Los Angeles, California

Southern Importers and Exporters, 4825 San Jacinto Street, P.O. Box 640, Houston, Texas

For dance footwear and tights the following places may be useful:

Capezio, 1612 Broadway, New York, N.Y.

Discount Dancewear, P.O. Box 22, Beverly Hills, California

Selva and Sons, 1607 Broadway, New York, N.Y.

When purchasing fabrics look at the wrong side as well as the right side: it might serve the purpose better. Many inexpensive fabrics on the market will give a very good illusion from a distance. Following is a list of some recommended fabrics and a few of their uses.

Unbleached muslin. Use it as is for linings, dye it for heavy drapable costumes, stencil it for pattern effects. It comes in several widths.

Percales, denims, and various other household cotton fabrics are excellent for shirts, skirts, blouses, aprons, and the like.

Corduroy as a velvet substitute comes in excellent colors and variable weights and prices.

Curtain marquisette, chiffon, and voile are good for sheer effects. The stiffness of these varies according to content: cotton, rayon, or nylon.

Osnaberg, terry cloth, monk's cloth, cotton flannel, suede cloth, or burlap are usable for heavy textured effects. Dyeing them will give a still different quality.

Jerseys knitted of wool, cotton, and some synthetics are excellent for flowing drapery. The cotton jersey has a tendency to cling to itself and doesn't drape as freely as other contents. Synthetic fabrics are rather unpredictable for dyeing—test a sample first. Costumes of the Greek and Roman periods and sculptured dance costumes are very good in jersey.

Leather is difficult to fake because the synthetic leather finishes are usually too stiff for costume use. Secondhand leather jackets and coats from thrift shops are excellent to recut into period jackets, belts, hats, and boot tops. If a tannery is nearby, ask for "splits." These are suedelike pieces of the inside of the hide and can usually be purchased by the square foot quite inexpensively. Hobby shop leather is normally too costly for the average school or theatre group.

For wigs it is not very satisfactory to try

to make natural-looking hair wigs unless labor is plentiful and skilled in wigmaking. However, many styles of nonrealistic wigs can be made of rayon horsehair, yarn, felt, raveled rope, and rayon or cellophane fringe. The synthetic hair falls sold for women can be converted into quite effective men's 18th-century wigs.

Armor, masks, crowns, and some kinds of jewelry can successfully be made of Celastic, a light durable synthetic fabric that looks somewhat like sheet asbestos. It comes in several weights, and when dipped in the solvent purchased from the dealer it can be shaped over a mold, allowed to dry, trimmed, bound, and painted. It dries very quickly, making it far superior to the old-fashioned papier-mâché. The medium weight, using one layer, is sufficient for masks, helmets, or jewelry. Two layers used for the breastplate and back of armor will make it practically indestructible. Binding the edges of the articles with a bias strip of Celastic protects it from cracking and bending. It will take any variety of paint.

Jewelry for stage use can often be a collection of cast-offs and broken pieces put together with heavy thread or fine wire to create a period look or special effect. Many inexpensive plastic jewels and beads also are available. For heavy chains, take a slow walk through a hardware store or the hardware section of a dime store. Many varieties of decorative chain are used in construction that can be gilded with shellac for very elegant effects. Jewels glued to Celastic-molded shapes will make pendants that can be hung from chain necklaces.

Selecting fabrics for period costumes requires extensive study of the period and a feeling for the look and authenticity of the clothing. Then select a modern fabric that will give this effect in draping, texture, and the way it will shape to the style of the costume. The quality of the fabric is less evident in a voluminous costume than it is in a form-fitting simple style. Often a costume full of ruffles can be effective with a much cheaper fabric than a form-fitting sheath dress. Fabric, plain and untrimmed, shows off its quality at considerable distance. Choosing the fabric wisely may enhance or detract from a well-designed costume.

Patterns and Ideas for Simplified Costuming. Skillful cutting of stage costumes is dependent on a knowledge of the shapes of the pieces that make up the total garment. Patterns can be purchased commercially only for modern garments, plus a few styles known as "masquerade" or "fancy dress" styles. These will sometimes work admirably for some costumes, leaving a wide variety of styles for which the only solution is to make your own patterns or adapt the available commercial styles. If one starts with a form-fitting pattern it can be enlarged for a loose-fitting garment, and with some experimentation and imagination parts of the pattern can be changed at will. If the personnel working on costume construction are reasonably skilled at sewing, they are accustomed to using commercial patterns and can alter size according to the instructions given. If the costumes constructed are going to be added to a costume wardrobe for future use, it is wise to increase the seam allowance to one inch and hem allowances to three inches in order to make them more flexible in size for future use. Fewer patterns are available for men than for women, and the average play has more male characters than female. Many pattern companies have a Colonial-style male and female pattern, and this is usable for a number of periods and styles with minor changes. Patterns for loose-flowing robes can be utilized for many unfitted garments. Trouser patterns are available for both sexes, together with some dance and clown costumes. Using genuine antique patterns when they are available gives the period costume an authentic look, but usually they make the construction of the costume much more complicated than the more streamlined modern pattern. It also takes more sewing and cutting skill to use them. If time is short and the labor unskilled, use the simplest possible patterns with a minimum of pieces. Rely on fitting the costume well and finishing it correctly for the final effect. The pattern companies listed below currently have some very usable patterns, as follows:

Butterick

3352	Santa Claus, coolie, Mexican, and doctor suit
3194	Choir robe
6765	Cassock for men and boys
9584	Centennial costumes, women and girls
3238	Variety girls' and misses' skating and dance costumes
3273	Variety girls' and misses' narrow skirt and pants types
3318	Colonial or Puritan lady
3319	Colonial and Uncle Sam man's costumes
3274	Devil, penguin, and space suit
3193	Animal suit
3169	Clown suit
5078	Boys' and men's Nehru jacket

Simplicity

6205	Girls' Colonial, Puritan, Southern belle, and frontier costumes
3294	Centennial costume and square dance costume and bonnet
6198	Boys' and girls' clown costumes
6201	Angel, fairy, witch and goddess costumes
6204	Ballet costume
7926	Men's Nehru jacket

McCall's

6514	Girls' witch, bride, fairy, and angel costume
2403, 2329, 2176, and 8942	Centennial costumes for girls and misses
9484	Men's or boys' Nehru jacket

Many very effective costumes can be concocted by using some simple basically shaped garments and then decorating them and rearranging the pieces for many produc-

tions. If a costume wardrobe is being built up, the use of it grows year by year as its size is increased. The costumes that get the most use are the simple shapes in assorted colors that can be put together in various combinations so they are not recognizable with repetition. When making garments for this purpose, finish off the necklines, sleeves, and hems; then, if trimming is to be used, superimpose it on the outside. Thus it is simpler for future use to change the decor without dismantling the garment. Putting trimming on by hand or with a long machine stitch also facilitates its removal. Making collars and cuffs separate, and temporarily fastening them in place, makes them interchangeable with other costumes.

Some of the simplest shapes, styles, and parts of costumes are shown here with a variety of possibilities for their use. The average period play will have a basic style of costume for women and one for men, and the differences in character will depend on color, variation in fabric, and decor. The styles here are those one finds in a great many plays, musicals, operas, and other theatrical productions.

The full-length leotard or leotard and tights combination for both men and women is an excellent basis on which to build dance costumes and those period costumes that follow the lines of the body. There are more historical periods of this type in which this can be used for men than there are for women. Seldom does a dance production aim at naturalism; it is more likely to want to suggest a period or an idea. The addition of a skirt, a shirt, a jacket, or accessories may provide just the right amount of realism for the audience interpretation. Plates IV, V, VI, VII, and VIII show some of the many varieties that can be achieved with this basic style.

The fitted-bodice, full-skirted dress for women is an excellent basic style, which is very adaptable. This basic dress tailored to men's measurements serves also for men's period skirted costumes. Patterns are given

PLATE IV Fig. 1

Basic style costume for dance; may be decorated for acrobats, trapeze artists, circus bareback riders, or draped with rags for witches.

PLATE IV Fig. 2

Simple chorus costume with short, medium, or long skirt. This may be trimmed with ribbons, flowers, borders, or left plain. The circular skirt is not only easy to construct but drapes well and allows maximum action.

PLATE IV

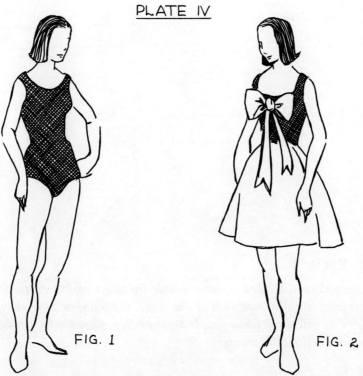

FIG. 1   FIG. 2

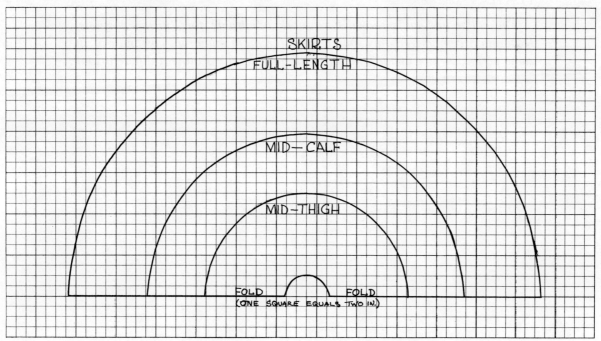

PLATE V Fig. 1

The long-sleeved leotard is more usable for most period costumes than the sleeveless one. With the addition of the short, medium, or long skirt shown on Plate IV, this will serve for a simple tight-bodice, flared-skirt period dress for choruses or individual characters.

PLATE V Fig. 2

The collar and cuffs shown here work admirably for Puritan costumes. Decoration can convert this simple dress for more elaborate costumes of the same period. A lace collar and cuffs will give the dress quite a different look.

FIG. 1

COLLAR

(ONE SQUARE EQUALS 1")

CUFF

PLATE V

COLLAR

(ONE SQUARE EQUALS 1")

FIG. 2

PLATE VI Fig. 1

The combination of tights and leotard or T-shirt can be used alone for dance costumes, or the addition of a simple jacket can suggest more conventional male attire. The addition of a belt will give a more dashing effect. This jacket can also be combined with the trousers or breeches shown on Plates XV, XVIII, and XIX.

Pockets, collars, cuffs, and trimmings would alter the appearance. The length of the jacket can be varied according to the desired effect. For example, a Spanish bolero ends several inches above the waist.

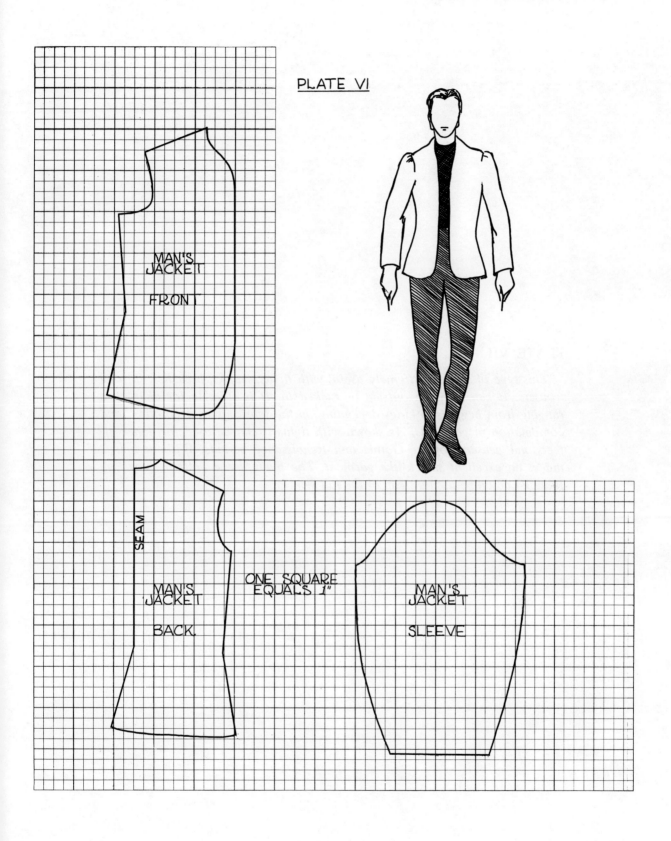

PLATE VI

MAN'S JACKET FRONT

SEAM

MAN'S JACKET BACK

ONE SQUARE EQUALS 1"

MAN'S JACKET SLEEVE

PLATE VII

This type of shirt is extremely useful with tights, trunks, breeches, or long trousers. It can be worn outside or tucked in. It is suitable for characters ranging from beggars to kings depending on the fabric used, decoration, and combination of garments. As shown with tights it can be used for dance effects and peasants of the Gothic and Renaissance periods. Without belt it makes an excellent smock-like garment. The plain sleeve pattern shown on Plate VI could be used instead of the full sleeve.

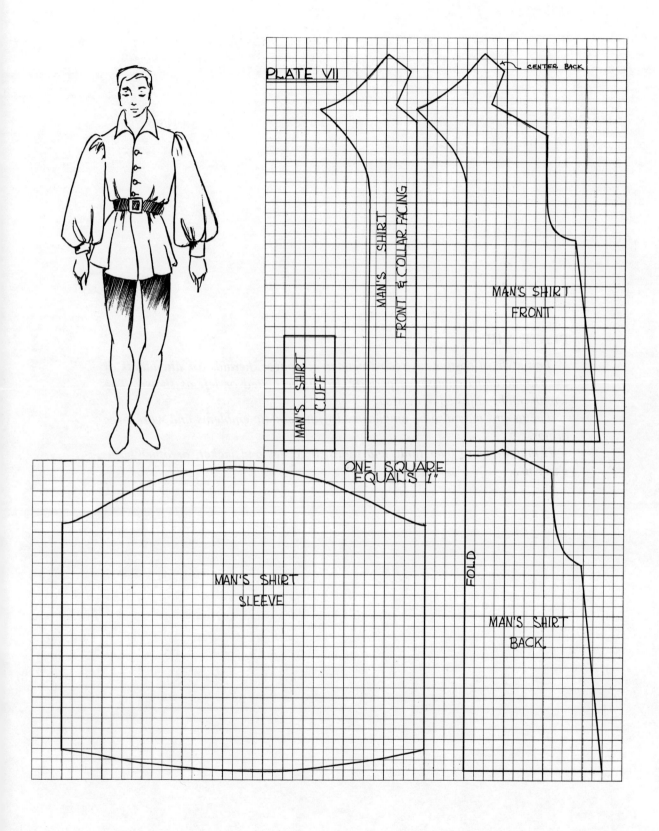

PLATE VII

CENTER BACK

MAN'S SHIRT
FRONT & COLLAR FACING

MAN'S SHIRT
FRONT

MAN'S SHIRT
CUFF

ONE SQUARE
EQUALS 1"

MAN'S SHIRT
SLEEVE

FOLD

MAN'S SHIRT
BACK

PLATE VIII

This style of costume is recommended for pages, heralds, or attendants of the Gothic and Renaissance periods. It can be belted or left as shown. The length can be adjusted as desired.

The tabard may also be emblazoned with heraldic emblems and worn over armor.

It may be worn over tunic and tights, breeches and jacket, or other basic garments.

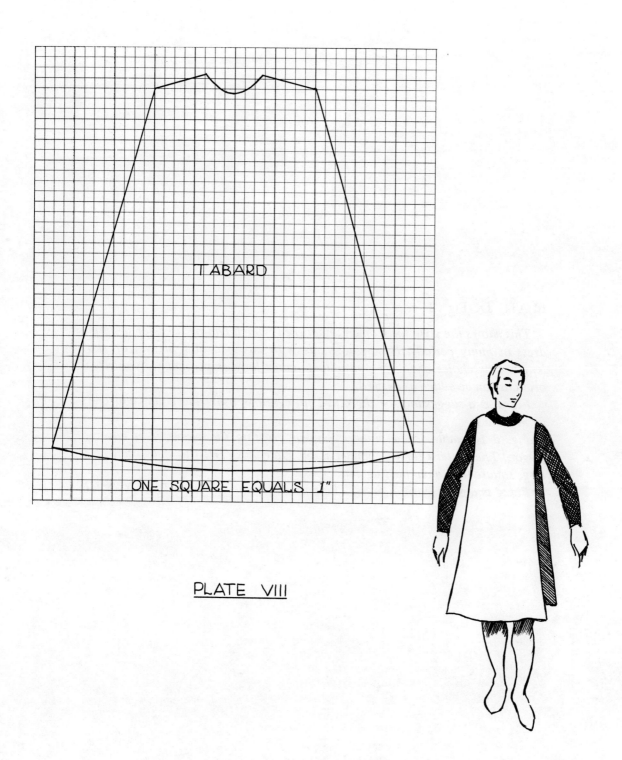

TABARD

ONE SQUARE EQUALS 1"

PLATE VIII

PLATE IX Fig. 2

This shows the style for women unadorned, which can be used for a simple dress in many periods. It can be made with any neckline, sleeve, or skirt length. The choice of fabric can indicate court lady or peasant woman. Decorations can be added as desired.

Fig. 1 is a suggestion for the mid-19th century, using the collar and cuffs from Plate V.

Fig. 3 is usable for a pioneer woman crossing the plains in a covered wagon. The pattern for the bonnet is on Plate XXVIII; the shawl can be a large square folded on the diagonal.

Fig. 4 is a good Puritan dress. The pattern for the cap is on Plate XXVIII.

PLATE IX

FIG. 1

FIG. 2

FIG. 3

FIG. 4

PLATE X Figs. 1-5

These show the pattern pieces for the dress illustrated on Plate IX Fig. 2. The skirt front gore plus four back gores will make a complete skirt. A skirt can also be made using three to five front gores or eight to twelve back gores. No seam or hem allowances are included. A center back placket is shown.

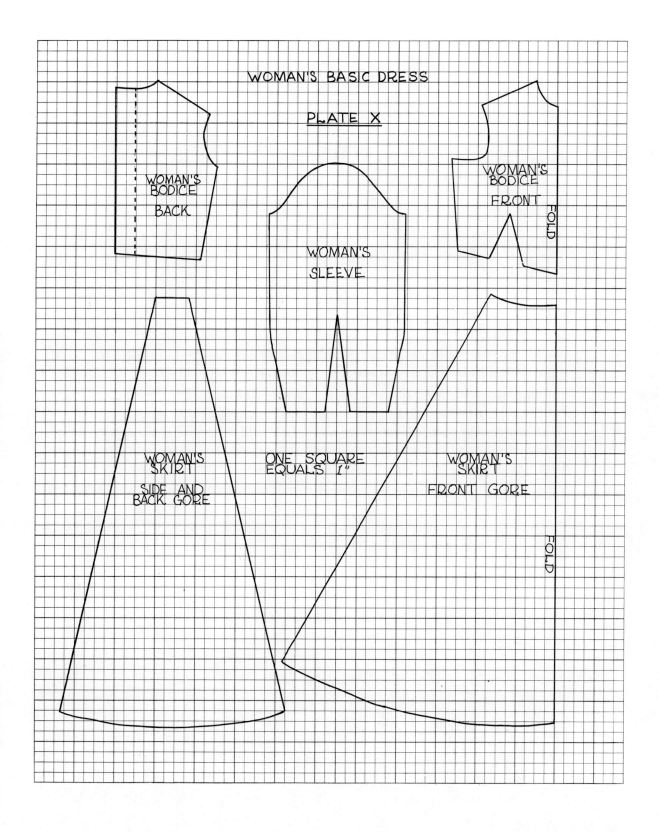

WOMAN'S BASIC DRESS

PLATE X

WOMAN'S BODICE BACK

WOMAN'S SLEEVE

WOMAN'S BODICE FRONT

FOLD

WOMAN'S SKIRT SIDE AND BACK GORE

ONE SQUARE EQUALS 1"

WOMAN'S SKIRT FRONT GORE

FOLD

PLATE XI Fig. 1

This shows the same dress with a double skirt and a shorter sleeve. This is a good idea for peasant dresses and may be used in several periods.

PLATE XI Fig. 2

This shows the skirt fullness pulled to the back and a front skirt drape for the bustle period of the 19th century. The shape for the skirt front drape is a semicircle arranged with the curved edge at the waist. The low neckline and short sleeve indicate that this is an evening dress.

PLATE XI

FIG. 2

FIG. 1

PLATE XII Fig. 2

The style shown is for a man's basic fitted robe or coat unadorned. This can be used for a priest's cassock, a long fitted Gothic or Renaissance tunic, or a dressing gown. Decoration can be added.

PLATE XII Fig. 1

This shows a necklace and belt added to give a more elegant effect. The Late Gothic hat pattern is shown on Plate XXIX.

PLATE XII Fig. 3

This is the same coat with fur additions and crown suitable for a king. Used with the hat of Fig. 1 it could be an elderly court gentleman. The pattern for the crown is shown on Plate XXIX. It can be made of buckram with the edge wired or with one of the newer products, such as Celastic or Polysar. Paint the crown gold; jewels may be glued on as desired.

PLATE XII

FIG. 1.

FIG. 3

FIG. 2

FIG. 4

PLATE XIII Figs. 1-5

These are the pattern pieces for the robe illustrated on Plate XI Fig. 2. Two skirt front gores plus four back gores will make a complete skirt. A skirt can also be made using three to five front gores or eight to twelve back gores. No seam or hem allowances are included. A center front placket is shown.

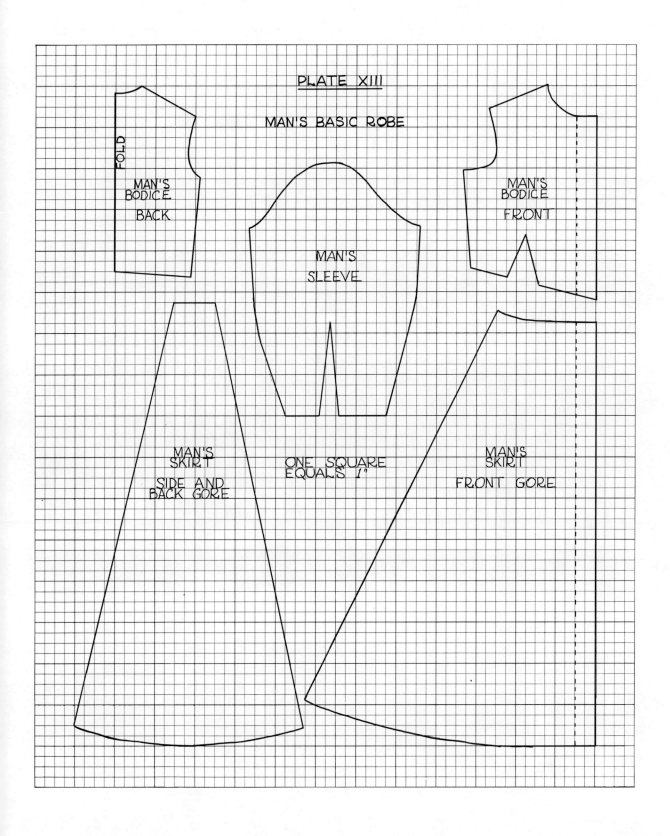

PLATE XIII

MAN'S BASIC ROBE

FOLD

MAN'S
BODICE
BACK

MAN'S
SLEEVE

MAN'S
BODICE
FRONT

MAN'S
SKIRT
SIDE AND
BACK GORE

ONE SQUARE
EQUALS 1"

MAN'S
SKIRT
FRONT GORE

PLATE XIV Fig. 1

This shows the robe shortened and laced, making a usable coat for a poor or wealthy gentleman according to the fabric chosen. This could also be made with the full sleeve pictured on Plate VII.

PLATE XIV Fig. 2

This is the same robe with a sleeve cuffed with a wide decorated band for variety.

PLATE XIV Figs. 3 and 4

These are the collar and cuff patterns for the garments shown.

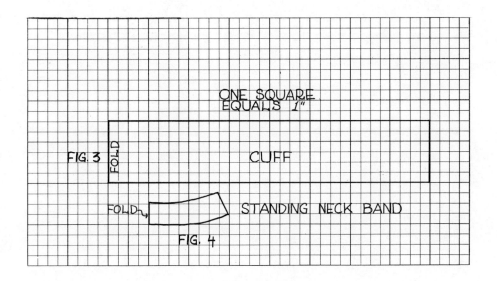

ONE SQUARE
EQUALS 1"

FIG. 3 FOLD CUFF

FOLD STANDING NECK BAND

FIG. 4

PLATE XIV

FIG. 1 FIG. 2

PLATE XV

This shows the full-sleeved shirt combined with long trousers and the pattern for the trousers and the sash. This is a good style for gypsies, folk costumes, and the dance.

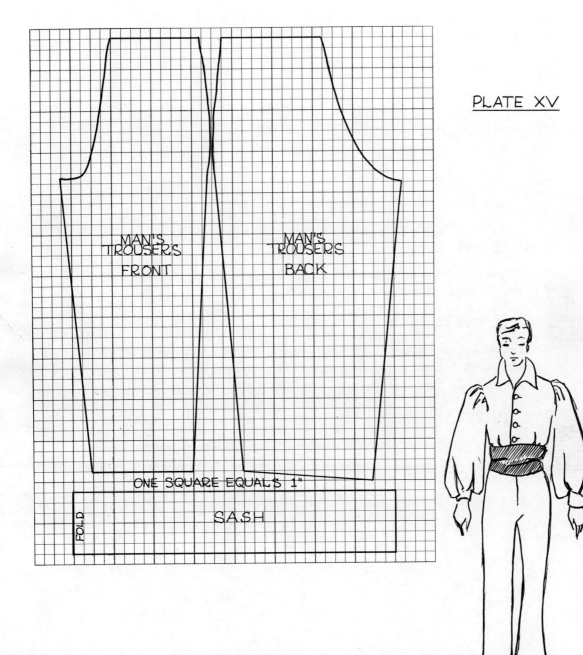

MAN'S TROUSERS FRONT

MAN'S TROUSERS BACK

ONE SQUARE EQUALS 1"

FOLD

SASH

PLATE XV

PLATE XVI

The full trousers shown here are different only in length. The same pattern is used for both and is shown on Plate XVII.

PLATE XVI Fig. 1

The jacket shown here is the robe pattern of Plate XII with a very short skirt. This outfit can be worn by Elizabethan servants or some Arabian Nights' characters. The pattern for the cap is on Plate XXIX.

PLATE XVI Fig. 2

This is another Arabian style combining the full-sleeved shirt with long, full trousers. The turban is a strip of fabric about 1' wide and 6' to 9' long, bound on the head as illustrated.

<u>PLATE XVI</u>

FIG. 1

FIG. 2

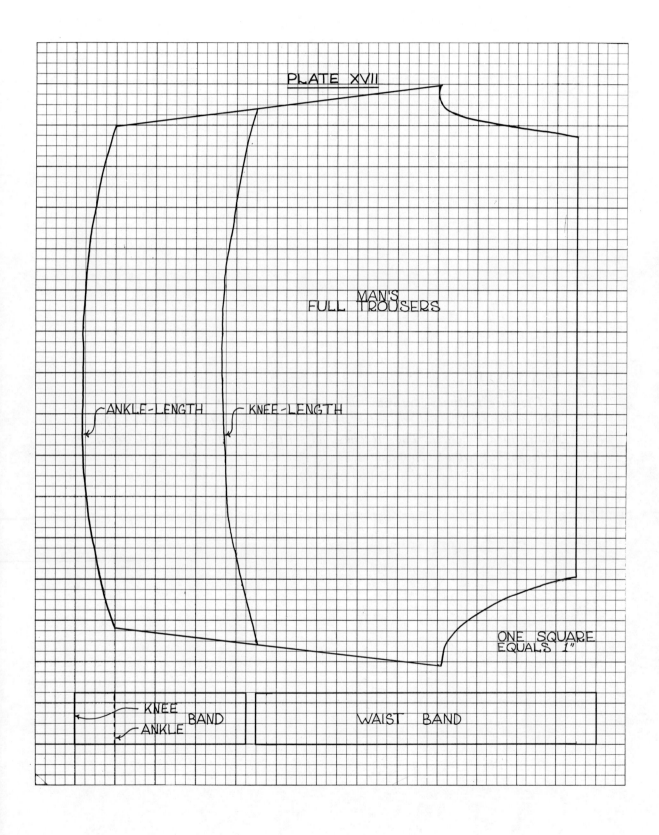

PLATE XVII

MAN'S
FULL TROUSERS

ANKLE-LENGTH   KNEE-LENGTH

ONE SQUARE
EQUALS 1"

KNEE
BAND
ANKLE

WAIST BAND

PLATE XVIII

The knee breeches illustrated are typical of the 18th century and some folk costumes. The pattern is for the moderately loose type. These can be tightly fitted if desired. The breeches and shirt combination is suitable for a 17th- or 18th-century commoner.

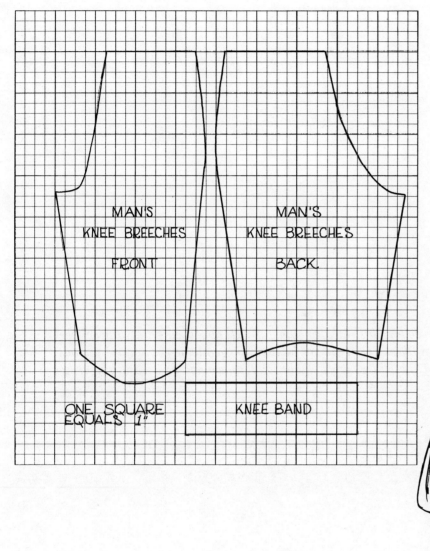

MAN'S
KNEE BREECHES
FRONT

MAN'S
KNEE BREECHES
BACK

ONE SQUARE
EQUALS 1"

KNEE BAND

PLATE XVIII

PLATE XIX

The same breeches illustrated on Plate XVIII are used here with a knee-length robe from Plate XII. This can be used for gentlemen of several periods. The addition of the collar, cuffs, jabot, and shoe buckles here distinguishes the 18th century.

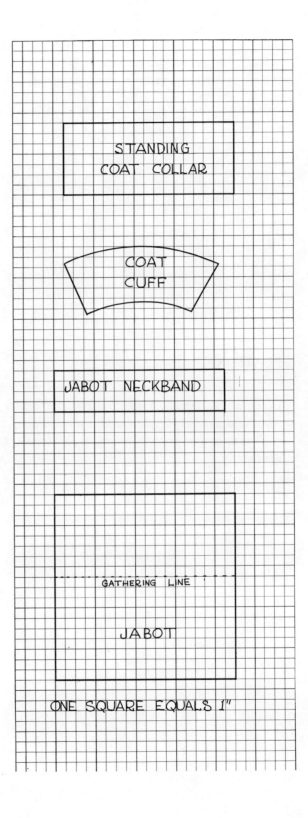

STANDING
COAT COLLAR

COAT
CUFF

JABOT NECKBAND

GATHERING LINE

JABOT

ONE SQUARE EQUALS 1"

PLATE XIX

PLATE XX

This illustration shows the same knee breeches with fitted coat typical of a Colonial gentleman. This coat has the center of the skirt back split to the waist and overlapping to avoid a separation.

This coat used with knee-length full trousers can be used for a 17th-century gentleman.

PLATE XX

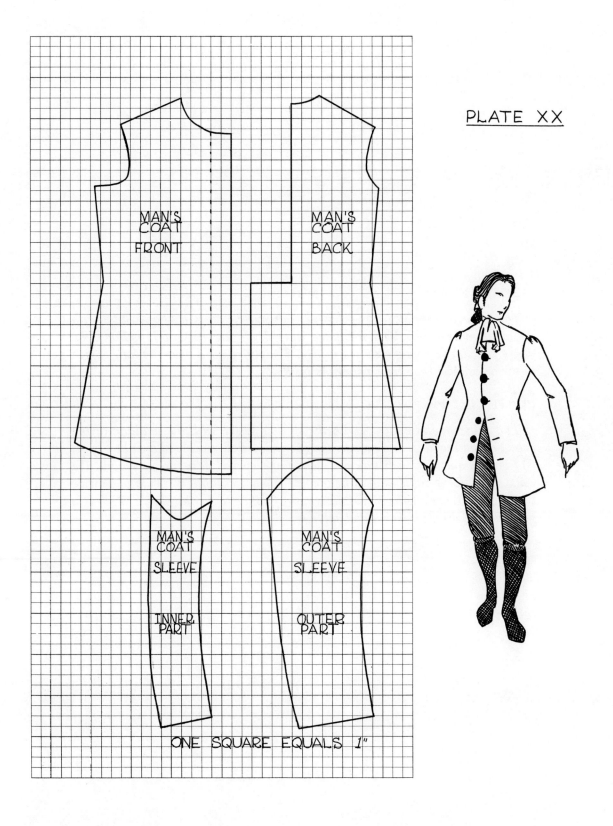

MAN'S
COAT
FRONT

MAN'S
COAT
BACK

MAN'S
COAT
SLEEVE
INNER
PART

MAN'S
COAT
SLEEVE
OUTER
PART

ONE SQUARE EQUALS 1"

PLATE XXI Fig. 1

The basic tight-bodice, long-sleeved, full-skirted dress is shown here with the addition of a collar and simulated wide sleeve for the Gothic period. The sleeve is a simple triangle shown in Fig. 3 superimposed over the long sleeve of the dress. The headdress pattern is on Plate XXVIII.

PLATE XXI Fig. 2

This shows the same dress with the shorter sleeve with the addition of the fichu around the neck and panniers at the waist. Patterns are shown in Fig. 4. Cut one pannier for each side and gather the curved edges to fit around the waist. The sleeve ruffle is a straight piece of fabric about 6″ wide and twice the circumference of the sleeve in length. Gather to fit the sleeve. This is a good style of dress for a Colonial lady.

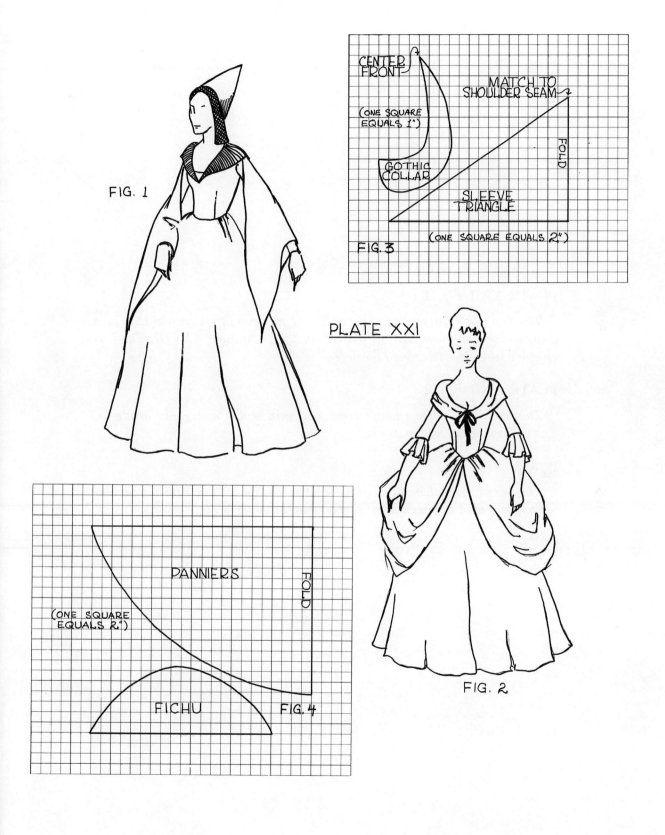

FIG. 1

FIG. 3
CENTER FRONT
(ONE SQUARE EQUALS 1")
GOTHIC COLLAR
MATCH TO SHOULDER SEAM
FOLD
SLEEVE TRIANGLE
(ONE SQUARE EQUALS 2")

PLATE XXI

PANNIERS
FOLD
(ONE SQUARE EQUALS 2")
FICHU
FIG. 4

FIG. 2

PLATE XXII Fig. 1

This is a peasant-style cap suitable for the mobcap of a Colonial lady or a dust cap for a charwoman. The pattern for this is on Plate XXVIII. The kerchief is a triangle used around the neck.

PLATE XXII Fig. 2

This shows the same triangle used as a skirt drape and gypsy headgear. The size can be tailored to its use.

PLATE XXII Fig. 3

This uses two semicircles as oversleeves to change a basic dress. A similar semicircle is used as a neck scarf. The pattern for this is in Fig. 4.

PLATE XXII

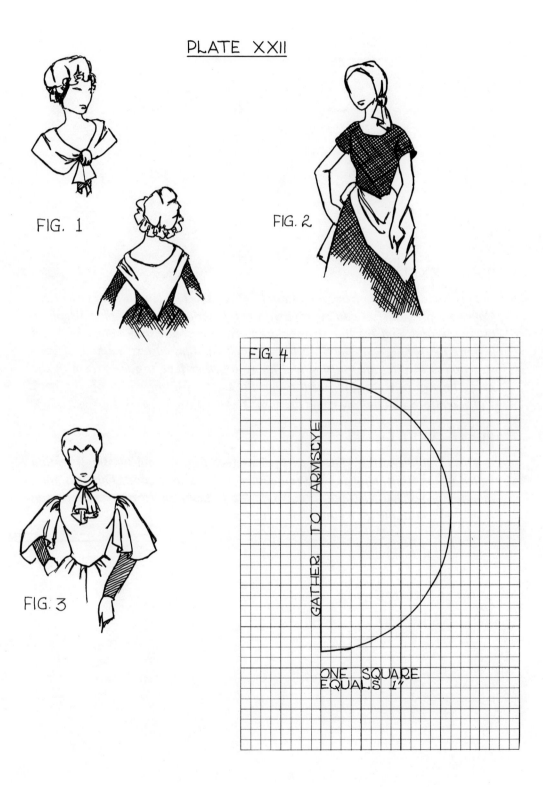

FIG. 1

FIG. 2

FIG. 3

FIG. 4

GATHER TO ARMSCYE

ONE SQUARE EQUALS 1"

PLATE XXIII Fig. 1

This is a cape made from a half circle (Fig. 3). The length may be varied. Capes of different sizes can be used with many period costumes plus disguises, outdoor wraps, and the like. If they are lined in a contrasting color the effect is more interesting and they are then reversible. The easiest method of construction is to stitch the outside and lining together face to face except at the neck. Then turn right side out through the neck opening, finish off the neck with a binding, and no raw edges are visible.

PLATE XXIII Fig. 2

This is another circle split in two places (see Fig. 4) and the small section belted in the front, allowing the remainder to hang as a cape. This is a good idea for pages, heralds, and attendants. Made from an elegant fabric it can be part of a costume for a court gentleman.

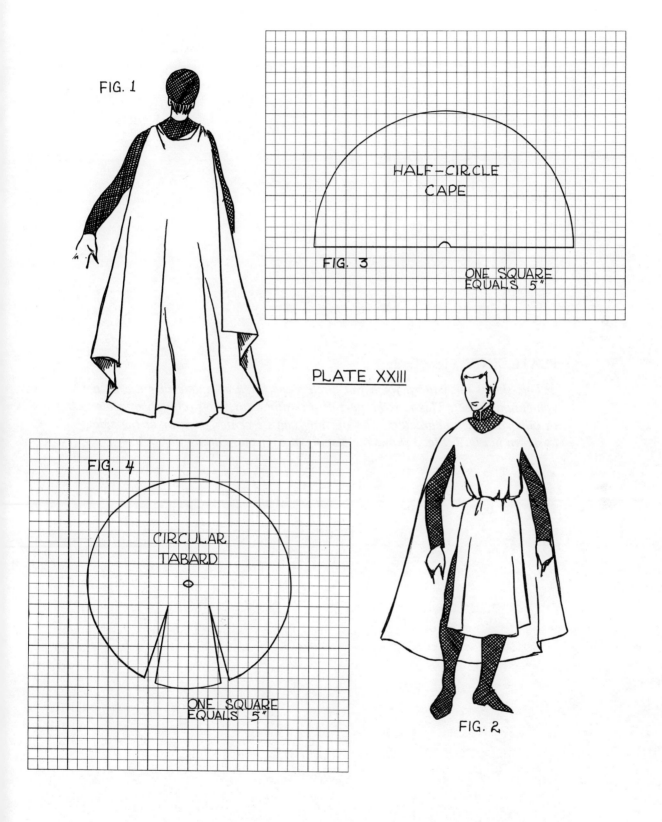

FIG. 1

HALF-CIRCLE
CAPE

FIG. 3

ONE SQUARE
EQUALS 5"

PLATE XXIII

FIG. 4

CIRCULAR
TABARD

ONE SQUARE
EQUALS 5"

FIG. 2

PLATE XXIV Figs. 1, 2, 3

This shows the pattern for a full circle cape for a complete disguise or a voluminous effect. This may be part of a costume for kings, church officials, or other dignified characters. The opening can be center front or at the side as shown in Fig. 2. Fig. 3 shows the placing of seams for cutting.

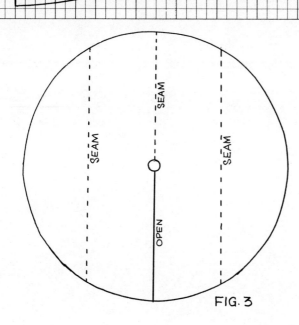

PLATE XXIV

FOLD

FOLD

FULL-CIRCLE
CAPE

ONE SQUARE
EQUALS 2"

FIG. 1

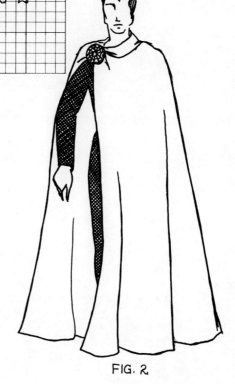

SEAM

SEAM

SEAM

SEAM

OPEN

FIG. 3

FIG. 2

PLATE XXV Figs. 1, 2, 3

This shows the variation on the tabard suitable for some ecclesiastical costumes or open-sided tunics. The solid lines in Fig. 3 show the pattern as illustrated in Figs. 1 and 2. Cutting on the dotted line could be done to achieve a broad-shouldered effect. The pattern for the mitre in Fig. 2 is on Plate XXIX.

<u>PLATE XXV</u>

FIG. 1   FIG. 2

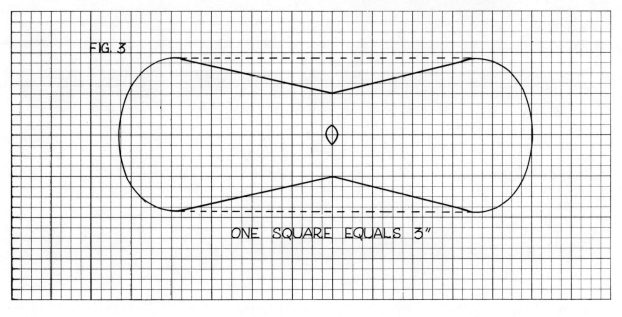

FIG. 3

ONE SQUARE EQUALS 3"

PLATE XXVI

This shows another usable shape as a type of cape, a train for a king or queen, or outdoor wrap. It may be worn over tunic and tights or even a long robe. A contrasting lining, fur edging, or other decoration can add to its elegance.

PLATE XXVI

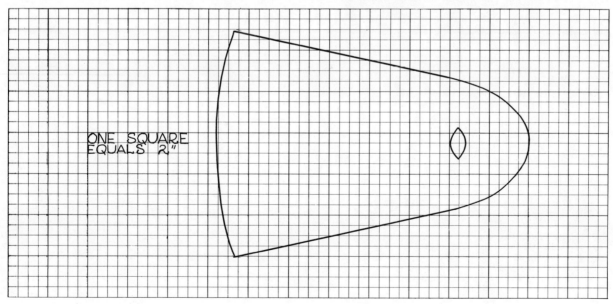

ONE SQUARE
EQUALS 2"

PLATE XXVII

A simple rectangle can be draped in many ways to provide dignity and elegance. Shown here is one draped in the manner of the Greeks and Romans. This can be used for allegorical characters, Greeks, Romans, narrators, and Biblical characters. It may be worn over leotard and tights as illustrated, plus long or short robes and tunics. Start the draping for this at the left foot front, proceed over the shoulder and diagonally around the body, ending at the left side in the back.

PLATE XXVII

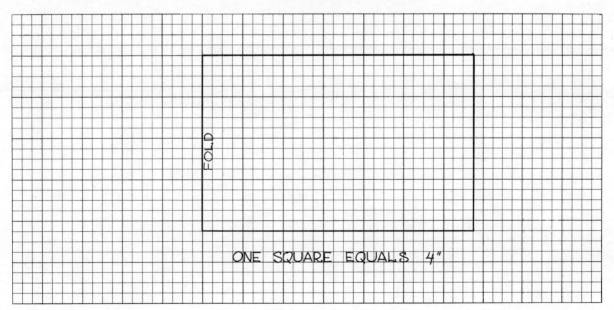

FOLD

ONE SQUARE EQUALS 4"

PLATE XXVIII

Women's caps and headdresses as illustrated on other Plates.

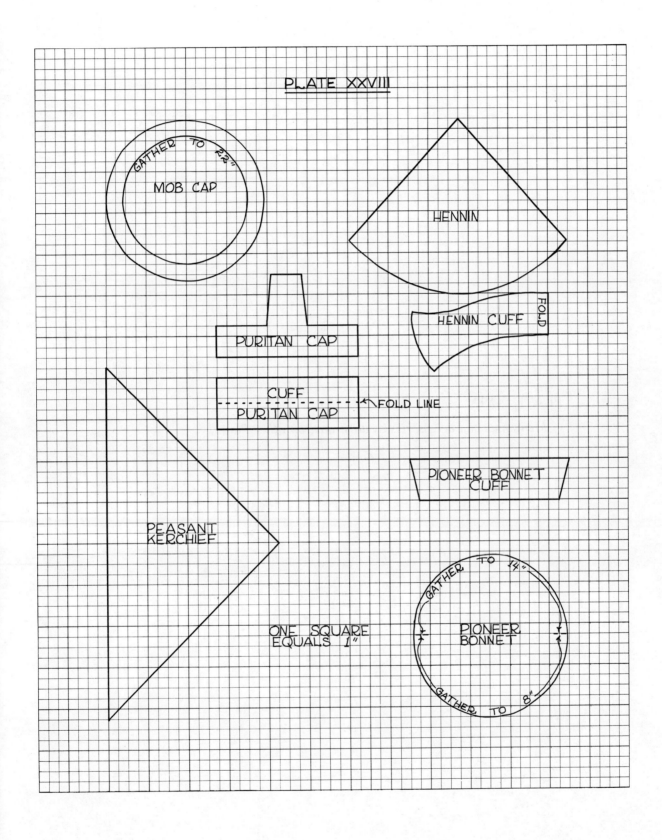

PLATE XXVIII

GATHER TO 23"
MOB CAP

HENNIN

PURITAN CAP

HENNIN CUFF   FOLD

CUFF
PURITAN CAP   FOLD LINE

PIONEER BONNET
CUFF

PEASANT
KERCHIEF

ONE SQUARE
EQUALS 1"

GATHER TO 14"
PIONEER
BONNET
GATHER TO 8"

PLATE XXIX

Men's hats and accessories as illustrated on other Plates.

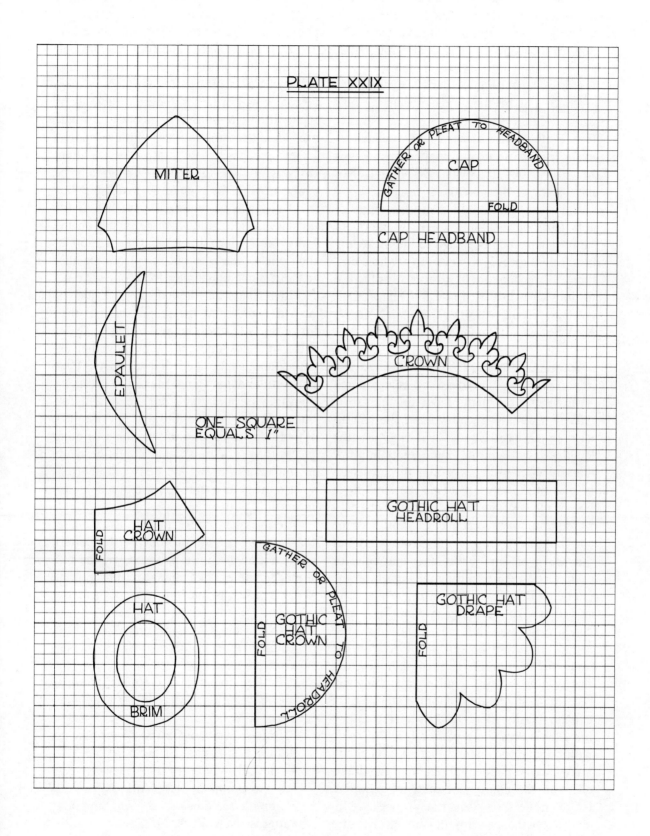

PLATE XXIX

MITER

GATHER OR PLEAT TO HEADBAND

CAP

FOLD

CAP HEADBAND

EPAULET

CROWN

ONE SQUARE
EQUALS 1"

HAT
CROWN

FOLD

GOTHIC HAT
HEADROLL

HAT

BRIM

GATHER OR PLEAT TO HEADROLL

FOLD

GOTHIC
HAT
CROWN

GOTHIC HAT
DRAPE

FOLD

here for both the men's and the women's measurements. Plates IX, X, and XI show the basic style, patterns, and ideas for variations of the woman's dress. Plates XII, XIII, and XIV show the same for a man.

For basic styles in separates, patterns are given for long trousers, knee breeches, a full-sleeved shirt (see Plate VII), and a jacket (see Plate VI), which can be used effectively in a variety of combinations. Plates XV, XVI, XVII, XVIII, XIX, and XX show some of the possible styles.

For some effects and many interchangeable parts of costumes, pieces of fabric in simple shapes can be added to the preceding basic styles or used to make up a whole costume. Given here are illustrations for the use of the shapes in varied sizes on Plates XXI, XXII, XXIII, XXIV, XXV, XXVI, XXVII, XXVIII, and XXIX.

Basic Construction Techniques. A few important things need to be remembered when laying the pattern out on the fabric ready for cutting. In most cases the lengthwise of the costume should also be the lengthwise grain of the fabric. Only in a few unusual circumstances would the crosswise or bias of the fabric become the lengthwise line of the costume. The draping of the fabric determines this, and most fabrics drape correctly along their length. Always lay out the whole pattern or estimate amounts for each piece before cutting any part of the garment. It is easier to rearrange pieces to save fabric before doing any cutting. Once cut, it cannot be restored. If the fabric has a nap or pattern be sure it all goes in the same direction on the garment. Napped fabrics or large patterns requiring matching will take at least one-third more material than a plain fabric. Plate XXX shows a layout for a basic dress on a plain fabric 36″ wide with no up or down, and Plate XXXI shows a layout on a napped fabric. Note the differences in the amount of material required. No seam, hem, or placket allowances are included on the patterns illustrated. Be sure

sufficient seam, hem, and placket allowances are made and that the measurements of the pattern have been checked against the measurements of the actor. Then cut the garment.

Where linings are required, use the costume part as a pattern for the lining. Stage costumes will fit better and hold their shape longer if all close-fitting parts of the costume are lined. Examples: tight-fitting bodice, knee breeches, close-fitting sleeves, tight trousers, tight skirts. This lining can be sewed in with the regular seams of the garment and acts to reinforce it further. If the outside fabric of the costume is laid on the lining fabric right side up and pinned to cut, then it is all ready to put the pieces together without detaching lining from outside.

Fitted parts of the costume should be pinned together at the seams, basted, then fitted on the actor before stitching. After fitting, the costume can be put together except for finishing hems and fasteners. Then fit it on the actor again, make the necessary adjustments, and mark for hems and fasteners. It can then be finished and trimmed. If there are shoes, headdresses, hats, or other pieces to be fitted also they should be ready at the same time as the body garments. It wastes the actor's time to have him come for more fittings than are essential.

The unskilled fitter should consult one of the sewing booklets put out by the pattern companies. These are published by the pattern companies and changed from year to year according to fashion. Some of them are:

Coats and Clark, *Sewing Book,* Educational Bureau of Coats and Clark, New York, N.Y.

Better Homes and Gardens, *Creative Sewing Library,* Meredith Press, New York, N.Y.

Butterick, *Short-Cuts to Home Sewing,* Butterick Company, New York, N.Y.

McCall's, *Tips for Easy Sewing,* McCall Corporation, New York, N.Y.

Simplicity Sewing Book, Simplicity Patterns, New York, N.Y.

Instant Sewing, Graphic Enterprises, Inc., New York, N.Y., 1968

Be sure, when fitting, that the actor is wearing the same kind of undergarments, padding, etc. that he will wear under the costume. Shoes of the correct heel height must be worn when hems are being measured. It is important to have the actor stand straight with the weight distributed on both feet. Avoid having anything within reach for him to lean on, then proceed as follows:

1. Have the actor put the costume on for the first fitting wrong side out. The costume will be in pieces: bodice, sleeves, trousers, skirt.

2. Line up the costume with the center of the body, clip armholes and neckline as necessary to keep the garment smooth on the body.

3. Pin together the edges of any plackets smoothly at the place where the fastening will later be installed. Keep this opening as straight as possible, particularly if a zipper is to be put in.

4. Let out or take in at the largest parts of the body first: bust, hips, upper arm, etc. Be sure any alterations made are symmetrical, take in or let out the same amount on each side. Alter each seam its full length, keeping the pins no more than 2″ apart.

5. Mark the desired neckline from center front to center back, allowing a sufficient margin for finishing the edge, then cut it. Use the cut-out piece for a pattern, mark the other half, and cut that. Refit the shoulder seams as necessary; frequently this is necessary when the neckline is cut.

6. Trim the armholes, if necessary, in the same manner as the neck. Cut one side, then use the cut-off piece as a pattern to cut the other side. Remember here, also, it will take a margin of about ½″ to finish off the armhole or to seam the sleeve in place. For a tight-fitting bodice with set-in sleeves be sure the underarm seam is pinned all the way up to the armpit. Cutting away too much under the arm will join the sleeves too low and make freedom of movement impossible. The garment will fit better if the sleeve is joined high under the arm.

7. Mark the bottom of the bodice with a line to show where the skirt will be attached or the bodice finished off.

8. To fit sleeves, put them on the actor wrong side out also. Pin them to the bodice at the underarm seam and at the shoulder seam. Ease the sleeve into place by straightening and bending the arm several times, pulling the sleeve up somewhat to allow for the action. Then alter the seams as necessary and recheck for bending action. Mark placket for length and placing before removing the sleeve from the actor. Time can be saved by fitting only one sleeve and matching its mate. When doing this, fit the right arm of a right-handed person and the left arm of a left-handed person.

9. When fitting trousers and skirts, get them adjusted and fastened at the waistline first to hold the garment in the proper place. Then work down from there on each seam. Again, be sure the sides are alike! Mark any plackets for length and placing.

10. Use tailor's chalk for all markings. Never use pen or other indelible markers. Plackets should be marked before removing the costume from the actor.

11. Always have the actor bend, squat, sit, or perform any action he will do in the costume before it is removed. If pins bend or come out, make adjustments and try the action again. This action test is very important with all garments. If the actor doesn't action-test the costume when being fitted, he may not be able to move when the costume is completed. It is easier to make adjustments at this stage than it will be later.

12. After the pieces of the costume have been fitted the first time, the costume can then be put together as a unit. It will need another fitting, which can be done with the costume right side out. Hems would be marked at that time plus placing of fasteners, trimmings, etc. Again, be sure the actor is wearing everything he is supposed to have

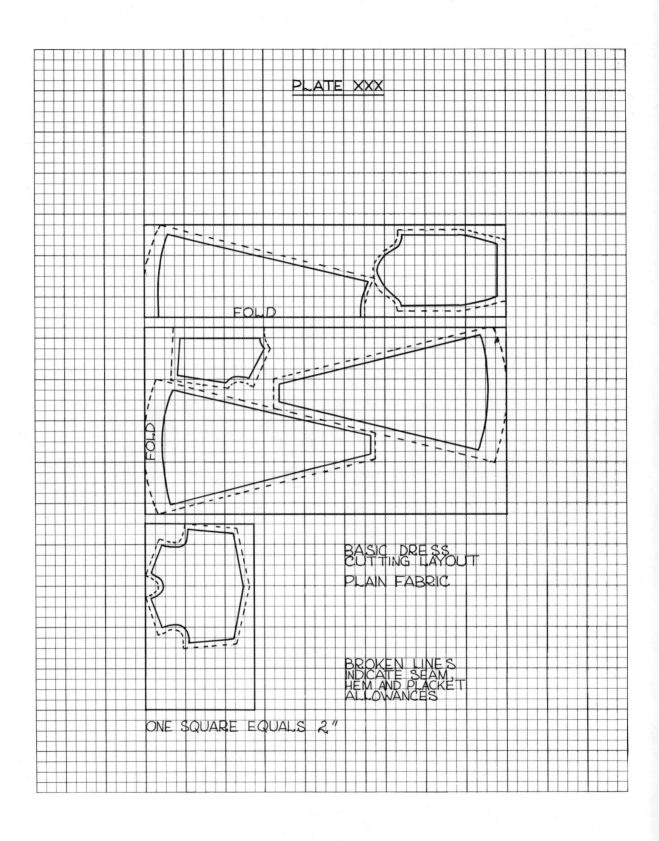

PLATE XXX

FOLD

FOLD

BASIC DRESS
CUTTING LAYOUT

PLAIN FABRIC

BROKEN LINES
INDICATE SEAM,
HEM AND PLACKET
ALLOWANCES

ONE SQUARE EQUALS 2"

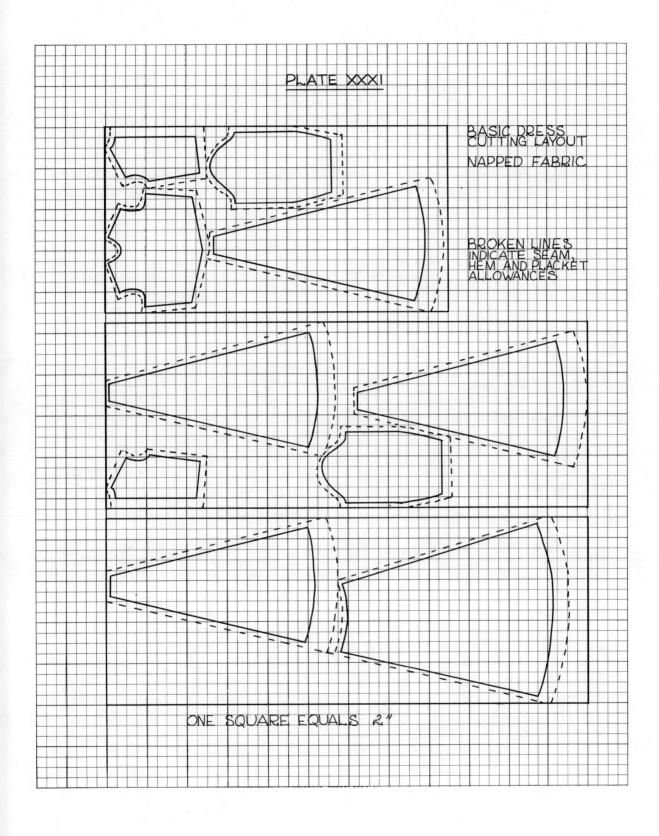

PLATE XXXI

BASIC DRESS
CUTTING LAYOUT

NAPPED FABRIC

BROKEN LINES
INDICATE SEAM,
HEM AND PLACKET
ALLOWANCES

ONE SQUARE EQUALS 2"

on under the costume and the proper footwear.

If one costume is to be worn on top of another for a fast change they should be fitted in the same way, one on top of the other. A tight-fitting garment can easily be worn under a loose one but the reverse doesn't work as well. Any costume that will have to undergo successive fast changes must be durable, fasteners must be secure and free from any loose threads or ravelings that would impede their function. This is particularly true in using zippers. An extra wide overlap on a zipper is less likely to get caught than the narrow one allowed on commercial garments. Also, if zippers are used in a period play a wide overlap will keep them invisible. They are a 20th-century invention and destroy the illusion when visible on a period costume. The zippers currently on the market, which do not show on the outside, are excellent for use in period costumes. Only the tag at the top needs to be hidden.

Following are some time-saving ideas that are useful for the costume construction process:

Using only black and white thread saves time in the threading and rethreading of sewing machines. For proscenium staging the audience cannot see the color of the thread used, so white thread for light costumes and black thread for dark ones serves very well. For arena staging it is better to use matching thread for any outside stitching on the costume.

When making a number of costumes alike, even though the sizes may be varied, they will go together faster if an assembly line is used for the construction. It is speedier always for a person to do the same thing over and over than it is to change jobs. An assembly line can be worked out using two or more people. The simplest technique is to work out the construction of the garment on a step-by-step basis, having only one thing done at each step—stitching, pinning,

pressing, etc. The time involved in each should be approximately equal, but this is not always possible. If some steps are longer than others, several people can work at that stage. Listed here is a sample step-by-step construction procedure for the man's full-sleeve shirt shown in Plate VI that can be cut in the proper sizes and would require no fitting en route.

Preparation. Look at the measurements of all the actors involved and figure out just how many different sizes are necessary. With the average group of adults three or four sizes will usually serve a rather large group: small, medium, large, with perhaps an extra large. Make a list of which actors get which sizes, and give each actor a number. Then cut the patterns for one-half the front, one-half the back, sleeve, collar, cuffs, and collar facing for each size. Include all seam and hem allowances and label the patterns prominently with their sizes, marking any edges to be placed on the fold.

1. This step needs a cutting table long enough to lay out at least a 9′ length of cloth, pins, good cutting shears, and tailor's chalk. With the patterns and sizes for each actor number (small—numbers 1,2,3,4; medium—5,6,7,8,9; large—10,11,12), have the fabric folded lengthwise and wrong side out, then fit the pattern pieces on the fabric properly, being as economical as possible. Number each piece of garment as laid out with the actor number so that there is a back, two fronts, two sleeves, one collar, two facings, and two cuffs for each number. With the fabric folded, the pairs of pieces will be automatic. Pin patterns in place, working from one end of the fabric, and mark around them with tailor's chalk. Remove each pattern piece after chalking and restack to continue using for other actors.

2. Cut out pieces as marked and stack in numerical order, keeping all the backs together, fronts together, etc. Keep sleeves and cuffs in pairs. Line up these stacks on

another table—backs and fronts side by side; sleeves, collars, facings, and cuffs on the opposite side of the table.

3. Pin back and fronts together at the shoulder seams, fabric face to face and the pins across the line of stitching, 2″ apart, all heads of pins on the open-edge side. Keep in the same numerical order and stack for stitching.

4. Stitch seams at proper width as pinned. The sewing machine should be within reach of the table where the work is stacked, and the stitcher should have a place to stack the work as each piece is stitched.

5. Remove pins and press shoulder seams open. The ironing board should be within reach to pick up the stitched articles and also within reach of a place to stack the work as finished.

6. Pin the collar back in place for its first stitching.

7. Stitch collar as pinned.

8. Remove pins and pin front facing and collar in place.

9. Stitch in place as pinned.

10. Remove pins and pin sleeves in place, matching the center of the top of the sleeve at the shoulder seam and adjusting small ¼″ pleats facing the shoulder on the wrong side. This will make a box pleat at the shoulder on the right side of the shirt. No gathers or pleats should be within 3″ of the underarm seam. Be sure to get the correct sleeves into the correct body by number.

11. Stitch sleeves.

12. Remove pins and pin ¼″-wide hem on each side of sleeve from the wrist end up 3″. This is the sleeve placket.

13. Stitch sleeve placket hems.

14. Remove pins and pin on cuffs for first stitching leaving ¼″ of cuff overhanging on each end.

15. Stitch as pinned and seam across cuff ends with ¼″ seam. This will make the cuff even with the placket hem.

16. Remove pins, turn cuffs right side out and pin for second stitching.

17. Stitch as pinned.

18. Remove cuff pins and pin side seams of shirt including sleeve seams down to the top of the sleeve placket hems.

19. Stitch these seams.

20. Press seams open after removing pins. Press a ¼″-wide hem all around the bottom of the shirt.

21. Pin this hem for stitching.

22. Stitch as pinned.

23. Remove pins and press shirt.

24. Measure and mark with crossed pins for buttons and buttonholes. Count out buttons for each shirt and pin onto the tail of the shirt with a safety pin.

25. Make machine buttonholes as marked.

26. Sew on buttons.

The step-by-step list could be used with any number of people or very few. As the first person completes all of his first job for all costumes, he can then shift to the end of the line and pick up the next job. The first worker needs a head start. It is important to arrange the traffic so that it moves smoothly around the room with no crossing of paths. If each worker is within reach of the next there is less traffic.

An assembly-line procedure works only when everyone sticks to his job. Coffee breaks should all be taken at the same time or one person can hold up the whole routine. It sounds complex to lay out work this way, but it gets routine work done much faster, and usually it is less tedious working in a group.

When all parts of the costume are completed, the actor should try it on prior to the first dress rehearsal. If an actor has several costumes it is a good idea to have him dress in each, in the order in which he wears them, for a final check at least several days before the first dress rehearsal. If this is done with all actors it makes for a smoother and less chaotic first dress rehearsal. Also, this final fitting can bring to light any deficiencies in the construction in time to correct them.

The designer should make out an itemized list of all parts of each costume after his designs are complete and early enough in the construction period to account for all details. This list is ordinarily part of the designer's construction details for the interpretation of the designs. This itemized list should be used at the final fitting and corrected if any changes have occurred in the interim. The designer must be present at all fittings. Then the list can be used to assemble and tag the costumes for each character. Large baggage tags hung on a hanger and listing the costume parts can be used throughout the run of the production. If there are dressing rooms where the costumes can remain while in use the assembled costumes can be put there. If the dressing rooms are temporary, have the costumes in a central place on racks and check them out to the individual actors. Spring clothespins are useful for fastening shoes together in pairs as well as labeling. An organized system of servicing the costumes with a costume crew makes for a smoother-running production. Keeping track of all the parts of all the costumes frequently is a major job, and replacing lost items isn't always possible. This depends on the reliability of the actors. Checking everything at the end of each rehearsal and performance is very good insurance.

Preceding the first dress rehearsal a costume parade is an excellent way of checking all costumes on the actors with the director. This may be done immediately before the first dress rehearsal or at a separate time. Ordinarily, immediately preceding the first dress rehearsal works very well. When the parade is completed, the rehearsal can get under way. This should be done on stage under lighting as close as possible to that used for the production. If the parade is not possible onstage, the costume designer should have one in the workshop or dressing rooms with the director. After the play starts to dress-rehearse the director finds it difficult to concentrate on just one aspect of the production.

During the dress-rehearsal period it is the job of the designer to watch his costumes in action and note any corrections necessary for their improvement. Any corrections noted should be completed before the next rehearsal in order to see the improvement. By the time of the final dress rehearsal all corrections should be completed and the production in perfect running order. The maintenance of the costumes must be kept up throughout the run of the show, pressing, cleaning, laundering, and repairing as necessary. It is important that the production look correct at every performance. It is a strong temptation to expend much effort getting ready for the opening and then to let things run downhill on successive performances.

Three or four dress rehearsals should be the minimum for most productions. The actors need these rehearsals to get accustomed to unfamiliar garments; the designer needs to see the costumes in use more than once; and the director needs to see the whole production put together to work out final details. If some parts of costumes are difficult to handle, either the garment or a reasonable facsimile should be introduced early in the rehearsal period for the actor to use. Items such as hoop skirts, long trains, and the like not only affect the movement of the actor wearing them but the movement of other actors onstage at the same time. Anything that is different from the actor's current clothing needs sufficient rehearsal for him to be able to handle the costume as if it belonged to the character before the play goes into performance. He will do a better job of acting if he is accustomed to wearing his costume.

After the last performance the costumes must be removed from dressing rooms or wherever they have been kept during the production and put away, returned, or stored. If costumes have been borrowed, they should be cleaned or laundered and returned promptly in order to preserve the good will of the people from whom they were borrowed. If costumes were rented, they should be packed and on their way back to the rental agency within twenty-four hours of the last performance. Delaying their return may result in an extra rental bill. Costumes constructed for the production that are to be stored must be cleaned or laundered before storing. They will deteriorate if stored soiled, to say nothing of the odor of stale perspiration. It is possible to save time and money by having the garments cleaned or laundered without pressing for storage purposes. They will no doubt need pressing in any case when brought out for later use.

Garments should be stored in as dry and dustproof a place as possible. An area where some costumes can be hung and others packed in boxes makes a good practical arrangement. Those garments difficult to press can be hung up, and shoes, hats, petticoats, shirts, and others easy to fold can be put in labeled boxes. A period classification plus the type of garment is the best method of labeling. Example: 18th-century dresses,

Gothic tunics. It is impractical to store a costume complete with underpinnings, hat, shoes, and accessories. Each part uses a different kind of space and it is unlikely that it would be used in the same combination again. It is wise to keep a matched suit together, that is, coat, vest, and trousers, or jacket and skirt. Other items store more easily according to the garment type. Most stage costume wardrobes have been started in a little-used closet and then expanded their space as the size of the wardrobe grew. Ideally, a dustproof room equipped with pipe for hanging garments and shelves with uniform-size boxes makes a very good storage room. However, few theatre groups start out with the ideal arrangement.

Many theatre groups find it useful to keep a record of the details of the production. A file of the itemized costume lists together with the designs, a program, pictures of the production, and the measurement chart can often be used as reference for wardrobe, publicity, or sometimes lobby displays.

After the costumes are no longer needed for the production, some theatres like to make a little money by renting them out to other organizations. Since there are licensed costume rental companies, individuals or amateur groups should not make a business of doing this without permission.

The wear and tear on costumes rented out is great and unless garments are sturdily constructed and will withstand repeated laundry and cleaning, it may not be worth the effort. Also, costumes will stand only a limited amount of alteration for the variations in size.

Sometimes a theatre may make arrangements with other groups for borrowing back and forth, with each organization using the costumes assuming any costs. There will always be laundry and cleaning with each use, and repairs and replacements when necessary. People normally do not have the same respect for borrowed costumes that they do for those they have made themselves.

A scene from The Wizard of Oz, *directed by Mary Kessler at Principia Upper School, St. Louis, Missouri.*

A scene from the staged reading of Dr. Faustus, *directed by Clayton E. Liggett at Spencer Community High School, Spencer, Iowa.*

A scene from Oliver!, *directed by Bert De Rose at Wilbur H. Lynch High School, Amsterdam, New York.*

A scene from Teahouse of the August Moon, *directed by Ernestine Smizer at Webster Groves High School, Webster Groves, Missouri.*

A scene from The House of Bernarda Alba, *directed by Joan Stroner at Alvernia High School, Chicago, Illinois.*

A scene from Oklahoma!, *directed by Julien R. Hughes at Leuzinger High School,* *Lawndale, California.*

A scene from A Comedy of Errors, *directed by Thomas C. Kartak at the Honolulu Theatre for Youth, Honolulu, Hawaii.*

One possibility with a school situation is for a school district to have a central dispensary for a costume wardrobe and each school check out its needs and contribute to the wardrobe in accordance with their productions. In this way one maintenance place and personnel could serve a number of organizations.

Costumes all completed for a production and piloted through the dress rehearsals and performances can give one a very rewarding feeling and self-satisfaction. Costuming a production is hard work even though it was envisioned as an inspired, imaginative activity. The problem of dealing with so many people and personalities can be nerve-racking. The director's changes of mind, the actors' fits of temperament, or helpers' failing to appear at the proper time make great demands on the time and energy of the person in charge. But it can be fun and self-rewarding also, the hours of working with pleasant congenial helpers, the coffee breaks with new friends as a result of the production, and the pleasure of seeing ideas come to life in color and fabric on actors on a stage.

A well-organized workshop can provide efficiency and calm among the help. If everyone knows exactly what he is to do, and his tools and materials are accessible, he will perform better and accomplish more. Workers sitting around idle while the designer figures out the next job or changes his mind may not show up when there is work to do the next time. Voluntary labor must feel useful and that they are contributing a share to the production. Actors will enjoy working on their own costumes and wear them in the play with more pride. In a community production, involving as many people as possible will create more interest and, in turn, increase the attendance. Some voluntary workers are excellent and knowledgeable and others are willing but not very skilled. Try to organize the work so that the unskilled can do the simple jobs and use the skilled workers where their skill is most needed. If the unskilled can become interested they will undoubtedly improve their skills. There is a myth that the technical side of the theatre production is done by frustrated actors or directors who haven't made the grade as performers. This idea discourages many excellent theatre personnel who have pride in their ability as designers and technicians. Prospective theatre workers sometimes feel that this is not an important phase of the production. No one part of a production is unimportant, nor is one phase complete without all the others. Actors, particularly, should have great respect for the costuming. The costume and makeup assists the actor in looking the character, lighting makes him visible and sometimes glamorous, the setting furnishes a background, and the director provides the movement pattern and correlates the whole production. A production is a cooperative enterprise and each area contributes to its success or failure.

Research Books. This is a selected list of some of the most useful books for stage costuming.

Arlington, Lewis C., *The Chinese Drama*. Shanghai, Kelly and Walsh, 1930.

Arnold, Janet. *Patterns of Fashion*. Wace, 1964.

Audsley, W. & G. *Designs and Patterns from Historic Ornament*. Dover Publications, 1968.

Barfoot, Audrey. *Discovering Costume*. University of London Press, 1959.

Barton, Lucy. *Historic Costume for the Stage*. Baker, 1935.

Barton, Lucy. *Costuming the Biblical Play*. Baker, 1937.

Blackmore, Howard L. *Arms and Armour*. Dutton, 1965.

Blum, Daniel. *American Theatre, 100 Years 1860–1960*. Bonanza, 1960.

Brooke, Iris. *Medieval Theatre Costume*. Theatre Arts, 1967.

Brooke, Iris. *Western European Costume*. 2 volumes. Theatre Arts, 1966.

Boucher, François. *20,000 Years of Fashion*. Abrams.

Collie, George F. *Highland Dress*. Penguin, 1948.

Crider, James. *Costuming with Basics and Separates*. Whitlock's, Inc., 1954.

Davenport, Millia. *A Book of Costume*. Crown, 1948.

Fernald, Mary and Shentow, Eileen. *Costume Design and Making*. Theatre Arts, 1967.

Grant, Francis J. *The Manual of Heraldry*. John Grant, Edinburgh, Scotland, 1962.

Grancsay, Stephen V. *Arms and Armour*. Odyssey, 1964.

Hansen, Henny H. *Costume Cavalcade*. Dutton, 1956.

Hope, Thomas. *Costumes of the Greeks and Romans*. Dover, 1962.

Joiner, Betty. *Costumes for the Dance*. Barnes, 1937.

Kohler, Carl. *A History of Costume*. Dover, 1963.

Laver, James. *17th and 18th Century Costume*. His Majesty's Stationery Office, 1959.

McCellan, E. *Historic Costume in America*. McCraie Smith, 1910.

McIan, R. R. *Costumes of the Clans of the Scottish Highland*. Stokes, 1845.

Mann, Kathleen. *Peasant Costume in Europe*. 2 volumes. Black, 1931, 1936.

Moncreiffe, Iain and Pottinger, Don. *Simple Heraldry*. Thomas Nelson & Sons, Limited, 1953.

Motley. *Designing and Making Stage Costumes*. Watson-Guptill Publications, 1965.

Norris, Herbert. *Costume and Fashion*. Dutton, 1924, 3 volumes.

Norris, Herbert and Curtis, Oswald. *Costume and Fashion*, vol. VI. Dutton, 1933.

Oxenford, Lyn. *Playing Period Plays*. Miller, 1957.

Payne, Blanche. *History of Costume: From the Ancient Egyptians to the Twentieth Century*. Harper & Row, 1965.

Prisk, Berneice. *Stage Costume Handbook*. Harper & Row, 1965.

Racinet, M. A. *Le Costume Historique*. 6 volumes. Didot et Cie, 1888.

Scott, A. C. *Chinese Costume in Transition.* Moore, 1958.

Warwick, Edward, Pitz, Henry C., and Wyckoff, Alexander. *Early American Dress.* Blom, 1965.

Waugh, Norah. *The Cut of Women's Clothes, 1600–1930.* Theatre Arts, 1968.

Waugh, Norah. *The Cut of Men's Clothes, 1600–1900.* Theatre Arts, 1964.

Wilcox, R. Turner. *The Mode in Costume.* Scribner's, 1944.

Wilcox, R. Turner. *The Mode in Hats and Headdress,* Scribner's, 1946.

Wilcox, R. Turner. *The Mode in Footwear,* Scribner's, 1948.

Wilcox, R. Turner. *Five Centuries of American Costume.* Scribner's, 1963.

Wilcox, R. Turner. *Folk and Festival Costume of the World.* Scribner's, 1965.

Magazines. The following magazines were started either in the 19th or early 20th century and are useful for those eras. Most libraries have some of them.

Delineator
Godey's Lady's Book
Harper's Bazaar
Ladies' Home Journal
National Geographic
Vogue